THE FLOWERING WAND

"If we want to locate the underlying source of our civilization's head-long rush to destruction, we must dig deeper than capitalism, deeper even than the Western worldview, until we encounter the bedrock of patriarchy. In this exuberant tableau of resurrection, Strand reveals how even our most archetypal myths have been molded and devitalized to fit the patriarchal straitjacket, and Strand lays the groundwork for a regenerated masculinity—one that is liberated to explore life-affirming possibilities grounded in the deep wisdom of long-buried ancient lore."

JEREMY LENT, AUTHOR OF *THE WEB OF MEANING*

"Sophie Strand's beautiful and poetic book is a game changer. With *The Flowering Wand* as a tool, it is possible to rewrite the mostly traumatizing patriarchal narratives Western males so often base their identity in and reconnect them with the underlying story of a cultural and natural deep history of mutual transformation with other beings beyond all modern binaries."

ANDREAS WEBER, BIOLOGIST, PHILOSOPHER, AND AUTHOR OF
ENLIVENMENT: TOWARD A POETICS FOR THE ANTHROPOCENE

"Sophie Strand writes with the urgency of a prophet and the musicality of a bard. Weaving myth together with botany, history with theology, her virtuosic linguistic skeins would do her beloved mycorrhizae proud. In *The Flowering Wand,* the masculine appears as lover, as partner, as inspirer, as friend. This is a book important in its joy, powerful in its love—exuberant in its curiosity. Taking us by the hand, Strand leads us into a garden of delights: tarot cards, ancient scriptures, Shakespearean comedies, sky gods, the Minotaur, the Milky Way. Strand holds the gates of wonder open and love comes flowing out. These are the birth waters breaking. Rejoice! The masculine is reborn."

AMANDA YATES GARCIA, AUTHOR OF
INITIATED: MEMOIR OF A WITCH AND HOST OF
THE *BETWEEN THE WORLDS* PODCAST

"A magnificent weave of ecology and myth—it is evident there's some pretty rich dirt, culturally speaking as well as actual dirt no doubt, under the fingernails that have written this lyrical journey. A book filled with magical insight, revealing Strand's wondrous curiosity and impressive learnings of the complex relationships between humans and nature."

SAM LEE, MUSICIAN AND AUTHOR OF *THE NIGHTINGALE*

"The wisdom in this book is almost beyond expression. Sophie Strand's *The Flowering Wand* reveals the full potency and profligacy of myth."

MANCHÁN MAGAN, AUTHOR OF
*THIRTY-TWO WORDS FOR FIELD: LOST WORDS
OF THE IRISH LANDSCAPE*

"Sophie Strand's work is a must-read for lovers of mythology and the Earth. Her work is poetic yet practical. It's whimsical and transportive, yet it's describing the world around you, inviting you back home to the reality of this mystical life and world we inhabit."

ANNABEL GAT, AUTHOR OF
THE ASTROLOGY OF LOVE AND SEX AND *THE MOON SIGN GUIDE*

"*The Flowering Wand* is a 'wild thing' and seeks out other forms of recombination and transformative fusion and gives them life. The surprising conclusion is, we humans have always been more-than-human. Are you wild enough to find out why?"

GLENN ALBRECHT, PH.D., PHILOSOPHER AND ENVIRONMENTALIST

"Sophie Strand's new book offers a luminous exploration of the radical mythic underpinning of the masculine narrative. Here the autocratic sky gods and sword-wielding dominators of people and landscapes are replaced by a dynamic ensemble of dancers, lovers, and liberators. Strand reminds us how these actors—from the Minotaur to Merlin—inspire people of all places and genders to break out of the straitjacket of patriarchal control and become more embodied, protean, dramaturgical, and emergent in our lives. Get entangled!"

CHARLOTTE DU CANN, AUTHOR OF
AFTER ITHACA: JOURNEYS IN DEEP TIME

THE FLOWERING WAND

Rewilding the Sacred Masculine

A Sacred Planet Book

SOPHIE STRAND

Inner Traditions
Rochester, Vermont

Inner Traditions
One Park Street
Rochester, Vermont 05767
www.InnerTraditions.com

Text stock is SFI certified

Sacred Planet Books are curated by Richard Grossinger, Inner Traditions editorial board member and cofounder and former publisher of North Atlantic Books. The Sacred Planet collection, published under the umbrella of the Inner Traditions family of imprints, includes works on the themes of consciousness, cosmology, alternative medicine, dreams, climate, permaculture, alchemy, shamanic studies, oracles, astrology, crystals, hyperobjects, locutions, and subtle bodies.

Cataloging-in-Publication Data for this title is available from the Library of Congress

ISBN 978-1-64411-596-1 (print)
ISBN 978-1-64411-597-8 (ebook)

Printed and bound in the United States by Lake Book Manufacturing, Inc. The text stock is SFI certified. The Sustainable Forestry Initiative® program promotes sustainable forest management.

10 9 8 7 6 5 4

Text design and layout by Kenleigh Manseau
This book was typeset in Garamond Premier Pro with Didot LT Std and Hello Paris Serif used as display typefaces

To send correspondence to the author of this book, mail a first-class letter to the author c/o Inner Traditions • Bear & Company, One Park Street, Rochester, VT 05767, and we will forward the communication, or contact the author directly at **sophiePstrand@gmail.com.**

Dedicated to the memory of my grandfathers,
Matthew Finn, Dave Tapper, and Mark Rogosin

Uplift the dark divine wand,
The oak-wand and the pine-wand,
And don thy fawn-skin, fringed in purity
With fleecy white, like ours.

. . .

Then streams the earth with milk, yea, streams
With wine and nectar of the bee,
And through the air dim perfume steams
Of Syrian frankincense; and He,
Our leader, from his thyrsus spray
A torchlight tosses high and higher,
A torchlight like a beacon-fire,
To waken all that faint and stray;
And sets them leaping as he sings,
His tresses rippling to the sky, . . .

EURIPIDES, *THE BACCHAE*

Young men, don't put your trust
into the trials of flight,
into the hot and quick.

All things already rest:
darkness and morning light,
flower and book.

RAINER MARIA RILKE,
THE SONNETS TO ORPHEUS

Contents

Introduction

The Sword or the Wand

Imagine that the great god Dionysus stands before you and rests his wand, *thyrsus,* on your shoulder. The thyrsus, wound with ivy, might be a woody stalk of fennel, unearthed from the ground, still dangling roots and a fine white threading of hyphae, dew-slick and perfumed with dirt. It erupts with leaves, fruit, and flowers. When Dionysus lowers his wand to touch you with it upon your shoulder, he will catalyze you into mystical ecstasy, and perhaps transform you into an animal or a plant. He is initiating you, not into a linear patriarchal narrative of knighthood, but into the gestalt consciousness of his chaotic, vegetal, polytemporal belief-sphere.

Do we want to hand the masculine a sword or a flowering wand?

The sword slices, divides, and subdues. Its tip drags imaginary borders across ecosystems. The sword does not embrace. It does not connect. It does not ask questions. It is not an instrument of intimacy. It either attacks or defends, affirming that every interaction is conflict, and every story is about domination and tragedy. The sword, perfected by the Romans as the *spatha* (or short sword) for the specific task of maiming and executing prisoners, quite literally cuts the mind off from the body. The sword proposes that we can wield our intellect without our somatic intuition and without our rooted existence in ecosystems.

The sword encapsulates the material reductionist idea that we can "cut" something up into discrete parts and thus understand it as a whole—that we must kill the animal to study the animal; that if we dissect enough brains, we might find the secrets of consciousness.

The wand, on the other hand, creates connections.

Some of the earliest examples of wands are the apotropaic hippopotamus tusk wands or "birth tusks" used in Middle Kingdom Egypt (1900 BCE), which were carved with lions, snakes, and frogs and used to magically protect pregnant women and children.[1] They are thought by some to have been used, specifically, to draw a circle of safety around a woman in labor. Inscriptions on these ancient wands tell us they are "the protector of night" and "the protector of day," which may indicate a belief that they helped establish temporal order. We also have the snake staffs of Aaron and Moses in the Hebrew Bible, which were used in spiritual debate, to part the waters of the Red Sea, and to draw water from a stone. These magical staffs that flicker between the solid and the serpentine flow into the healing caduceus of Hermes, a winged wand encircled by two snakes. Rhabdomancy, or dowsing, once used forked wooden wands to magically survey the land for water, a practice that may date back nearly eight thousand years, as evidenced by art in the Saharan Tassili caves. Homer makes numerous references to magical wands in both the *Iliad* and the *Odyssey*, putting them in the hands of Circe, Athena, and Hermes. Celtic mythology also features many wands, rods, and staffs; for example, in the famous legend of Fionn MacCumhaill, the hero uses hazel wands to transform people into animals, as a divination device, and to defend himself from harm.

The wand encircles us with protection during biological rites of passage from birth to marriage to death. It draws us to water. It enchants us into closer kinship with animals and plants and landscapes by literally transforming us into them. It mends broken bodies, knits wounds, and softens minds hardened by anthropocentrism.

While swords are made only by human hands, wands, it may be argued, predate human beings themselves. All it takes is a woody shoot bursting into blossom. A cedar branch. A sprig of hawthorn. A tree erupting in lichens. For that very reason, perhaps, wands have been central to magical and ritual practices since before human history began to be recorded.

When I began my research into the myths most responsible for our understanding of masculinity today, I discovered that the masculine hadn't always been conflated with the violence of hierarchy and domination. Long before the sword-wielding heroes of legend readily cut down forests, slaughtered the old deities, and vanquished their enemies, there were playful gods, animal-headed kings, mischievous lovers, vegetal magicians, trickster harpists, and riddling bards. These archetypes of ancient masculinities are mirrored by contemporary discoveries in biology, genetics, ecology, and quantum physics. My deepening study into myth and science blurred my ideas of gender distinction and, even more excitingly, my ideas of bounded individuality.

In rewilding the myths of the masculine, we must understand that myths were originally situated in particular ecosystems. Just as mushrooms are the fruiting bodies of underground mycelia, so are myths the aboveground manifestations of specific ecologies. Myths are momentary eruptions of beings that have been growing for millennia belowground.

As a mythic figure, "Orpheus" is now understood to have been a title rather than a single character, and lyric prophets through the centuries stepped into the role of the divine lyrist to sing his Orphic hymns. Dionysus, the god of the vine, appears without warning, throwing cities into disorder. Although archaeological evidence shows that he is one of the oldest pre-Olympic gods, he is, paradoxically, personified as a "newcomer" or "stranger." Dionysus fruits up across the Mediterranean in different cities, often with a different appearance, offering a variety of fermented beverages. But the real Dionysus is the mycorrhizal system of vegetal gods, weaving a net that is ready to pop up and proliferate wherever nature-based, ecstatic wisdom is needed.

Our textual myths are the fruiting bodies of these vegetal gods.

And when we have a fruiting body, we must ask: Where are its roots located? What is its mythic mycelium? Where has it come from? If we fail to address these questions, we are doomed to misunderstanding and confusion.

Nowhere is this made more clear than in the case of the illiterate magician and storyteller known as Jesus. He has been deracinated from the ecology of Galilee by the empire that later embraced him. Unlike the vegetal gods Osiris and Dionysus before him, his body did not go back to the forest floor to nourish the fungi and complete the virtuous cycle of decay and renewal. Instead, after his resurrection, he ascended into heaven. His body was literally "disappeared." No wonder his teachings have been perverted into simplistic dogma. Jesus himself is no longer even connected to the earth.

Plants first made their way onto dry land some 416 million years ago. But these were not the sturdy trees and sessile flowers we know today. They had no roots. Instead, fungi kept these earliest plants plugged into nutrients and set in place for millions of years before the two developed a converged evolution. Plants "learned" to have roots from fungal networks that predated them by over half a billion years.[2]

Mushrooms, visible aboveground, are the momentary expression of fungi that live most of their life belowground as branching, threadlike webs called mycelia. These mycelial life-forms grow and explore the soil and connect ecosystems by way of filamentous tubes called hyphae that grow cell by cell.

Just as fungi originally taught plants how to root into the soil, so myths teach us how to root into relation with our ecological and social ecosystems. They narrativize a deep understanding of our connection to more-than-human time scales.[3] As the poet Robert Bringhurst has pointed out, myth isn't antagonistic to science but rather an alternative science in itself. He observes, "[Myth] aims, like science, at perceiving and expressing ultimate truths. But the hypotheses of myths are framed as stories, not as equations, technical descriptions, or taxonomic rules." While a scientist quantifies reality, he explains, a myth teller personifies it.[4]

But now we are living in a strange time in which most of our myths are deracinated. We think we have myths, but really these stories are like houseplants, cut off from the complexity of rhizome and soil and therefore unable to refruit as something freshly adapted to our current environmental conditions and social circumstances. "Because mythologies and sciences alike aspire to be true, they are perpetually under revision," Bringhurst explains. "Both lapse into dogma when this revision stops."[5]

Revision is decay. It is the acknowledgment that most of the work happens underground. Dionysus understands that he must be a different mushroom in Crete than he will be in Thrace. Our myths must have root systems they can sink back into to revitalize the soil, reemerging with the magic particularly suited for this age of ecological chaos.

Each myth is the mushroom of a certain place, an eruption suited to a specific patch of moss, sulfur deposits, decaying wood, and forest floor. These mythic eruptions are the moments when a culture senses the need to spread, to find new food, to shift direction. They are reproductive flourishes. Entering into the open air, they sporulate old knowledge in new ways. A hero is not an individual. A hero is a reproductive event.

Our bodies, it turns out, are swarms of aliveness, composed of microbes and fungi, metabolically dependent on plants and animals for sustenance, and wildly, generatively entangled with our landscapes and communities. And these bodies—our bodies—are suffering. Men. Women. And every sacred expression in between. Patriarchy's monolithic vision of the masculine is bad for everyone and terrible for our ecosystems.

But patriarchy is not the only narrative. Wilder, more magical modes of the masculine have always been hidden just below our feet, and just below the surface in stories and folktales we think we understand. But we need to trace them back into the earth. We need to re-root the stories and myths we think we know back into their ecological and social contexts.

There is an underworld below us, where fungi-like systems have sequestered ancient wisdom, keeping its soil safe from exploitation. The time has come to access the biodiversity that still lives secretly in the root systems of familiar myths. Recovering an efflorescence of expressions of the mythic masculine can help us confront patriarchy's devastating effects on the environment and construct a new way forward in an age of crisis. What is masculinity? What has it meant in the distant past? What could it mean?

The flowering wand affirms the holarchic nature of reality: we are matryoshka dolls of being, simultaneously composed of worlds and constituting larger worlds, systems that can be understood only in their connective plurality, rather than when broken down to parts.* This view, only recently accepted in mainstream science, is central to most Indigenous belief systems. Ethnobotanist Enrique Salmón uses the term *kincentricity* in relationship to the work of community organizer and conservationist Dennis Martinez to explain the way his Indigenous knowledge-based approach to resilient ecosystems and ecological restoration differs from material reductionist ecosystem management.[6] Complexity and relationships are key to reciprocal understanding and to cultivating biodiversity that can withstand shifting climatological pressures and anthropogenic incursion. Our relationships, our webs of kinship, are what will save us as we confront climate change. I see the wand illuminating that invisible connective tissue that creates a living, breathing world, drawing kinship between flora and fungi and fauna into focus.

The sword, held in the other hand, seems a fitting symbol of the Anthropocene. Think of the most powerful sword of them

---

*The term *holon* refers to something that is a whole in and of itself, while also belonging to a larger whole. In his 1967 book *The Ghost in the Machine,* Arthur Koestler coined the term *holarchy,* meaning a system of interacting holons, in which each holon is both a part and a whole, to explain the universe's tendency to integrate individual organisms into more complex systems. How can we think of our bodies as ecosystems of kinship? How can we see ourselves as relationally woven into the larger whole of our environment?

all: Excalibur, pulled by King Arthur from a stone. But pause. Examine the hilt surfacing from a huge boulder. The shaft glistening before disappearing into the mute solidity of rock. What are we looking at?

We are not just looking at a sword. We are looking at a stratigraphic penetration of the human into the earth. For how does a sword get into stone? Time. It takes thousands of years and sediment to swallow the blade. If the Anthropocene is constituted as a convergence of scales— the human and the geological—then the image of the sword in the stone would seem to be the best example. The human has ruptured linear temporality. He has stuck his "blade" deep into the tectonic layers of polytemporality.

Arthur takes the sword out of the stone in order to fight and prove his kingship—his "dominance" over other beings. Perhaps, then, we should put the sword back in the stone, letting it fossilize and become a monumental reminder of this time when we cut ourselves off from the land, the animals, the plants, and our interrelated ways of knowing.

Let us give back to the masculine the flowering wand—the thyrsus. Let him find the water in the land so he can protect it. Let the masculine use his wand to pour himself into other modes of consciousness so he can develop a matured ecological empathy. With the wand he does not have to prove anything through force. His job is to connect, to close wounds—his own and the wounds of other beings and landscapes. As he uses the wand, he will feel its vines begin to snake into his own veins, the magic of the world reinvigorating his own sluggish circulation. And then he, too, can flower alongside his wand, outward, into a power that is soft, curious, connective, and celebratory.

～

A single voice cannot hope to encompass the biodiversity of the world's perspectives and ecosystems, and so the aim of this book is not to be comprehensive but to represent an invitation.

I am of European descent, raised in a family that, through heritage, conversion, and marriage, celebrated Christian, Buddhist, Jewish, and Pagan spiritual traditions. I was raised on folk and fairy tales, myths and legends, the stories of the Bible, and the fantasies of C. S. Lewis and J. R. R. Tolkien.

I was also raised in the shadow of mountains and the shade of oak trees, hemlocks, and white pines, alongside coyotes, raccoons, skunks, snapping turtles, and bears, with ferns and mushrooms.

That I do not have an intimate, ancestral, or ecological knowledge of the folktales and myths of, say, Japan or Ecuador or Kenya does not mean they don't deserve to be celebrated and rewilded. Rather, this book is an invitation for everyone to collaborate on the storytelling work of rewilding the masculine. Storytelling, historically, has been an oral and collaborative process.

My greatest desire is to be in conversation with you.

PART I

BACK TO THE ROOTS

1

Sky, Storm, and Spore

Where Do Gods Come From?

Behold, the Lord hath a mighty and strong one, which as a tempest and a destroying storm, as a flood of mighty waters overflowing, shall cast down to the earth with the hand.

ISAIAH 28:2 (KING JAMES VERSION)

The God of the Old Testament is, above all else, a storm god. He speaks to Job from "out of the whirlwind" (Job 38:1). He precipitates the flood that extinguishes all life except for the beings in Noah's ark. Perhaps his worst punishment is the withholding of storms altogether, causing fatal droughts. The prophet Elijah, when he finally summons God, summons not a man or a cosmic figure but, curiously, "a little cloud . . . like a man's hand" (1 Kings 18:44).

Yahweh is not the only storm god. The Yoruba goddess Oya causes tempests. Thor wields his lightning bolt, as do Zeus and the Celtic god Taranis. Tamar releases the rains in Georgia, and Bunzi is honored by the Kongo people for bringing the monsoons. Isis and Osiris work together, in Egypt, to summon the river-swelling rains that will irrigate farm fields. One of the oldest gods is Indra, the Vedic god of storms, lightning, rain, and rivers. Scholars of Indo-European mythology hypothesize that he could be the root of other thunder deities such as Thor, Zeus, and Perun.

Before the age of weather satellites, storms were capricious—sometimes a miracle, sometimes a cataclysm, and generally unpredictable. Rains can wash away civilizations, but they also feed them, nourishing the fields of grain that will be baked into life-affirming bread. No wonder storms were seen not only as the work of the divine, but as the very manifestation of the divine itself. Lightning knifes through thick air, splitting a sycamore in two. Sheets of silver water waft from the heavens. Clouds bloom from the sky, violet and hurt, like a bruise on the skin.

Storms appear to inhabit the sky, but they are also intimately involved with landscape. They kick up sand tornadoes and twist seas into cyclones. They overflow rivers with fallen trees and debris, and intimately carve their inhuman stories into the landscape. So, while they fly and swoop through the heavens, storm gods are still elemental; they are still embodied.

Sky gods, on the other hand, are fully evaporated and unanchored. Storm gods, predating monotheism, don't start as sky gods, but they quickly become them. Sky gods are not made of water and sand and fire and wind. They cannot even be imagined. They are separate from the world and its chaotic weather. This spiritual distancing opens up space for the very abstraction that will let humans understand themselves as separate from their ecosystem.

But what if I told you that storm gods don't come just from the sky? They also come from underground.

Research into cloud formation and rainfall has yielded interesting results. One of the drivers behind rainfall is something very curious indeed: fungal spores. The group of fungi that produce mushrooms, called basidiomycetes, grow through an osmotic inflation process, their hyphae bonding together and filling with water in order to "bloom" above the soil.[1] Once the mushrooms have developed, tiny stalks (basidia) grow underneath the mushroom cap, culminating in tiny spores. A drop of water forms between the gills under a mushroom's cap. Finally, the water droplet condenses against the spore, jettisoning the spore out of the mushroom. In his book *Mycelium Running: How Mushrooms Can Help Save the World,* mycologist Paul Stamets estimates that the force with which mushrooms eject spores is ten thousand times the force undergone by astronauts as they exit the gravitational pull of Earth's orbit.[2] Some land many inches away from the original mushroom. But most are buoyed upward by the wind, into the sky.

Spores are practically invisible, a shimmer of dust, vaporous. But while they are tiny, they are numerous. More numerous than just about any other organic component in the atmosphere. Every year, around fifty million tons of spores enters into the atmosphere. Some of those spores will immediately land in the dirt and begin, hypha by hypha, to root into the underworld. But millions of tons of spores do something else entirely. Some make it fifty miles up into the air and ride the currents for weeks. They follow the wind. And, like the storm gods, they generate rain.

Sugars on the spores' surface cause water to condense around them once they have been ejected. Spores become a nucleus of sorts in a floating water molecule. These water-coated spores bump into each other, again and again, millions of times, until they accumulate into rain clouds.

In experiments conducted in closed laboratory settings with a variety of different mushrooms, spores created an atmosphere with a relative humidity between 101 and 102 percent, the same oversaturation conditions found in clouds. Researchers concluded that fungi are a key part of a feedback loop in forests and rainy regions.[3] Fungi need damp environments in order to fruit up into reproducing mushrooms. These mushrooms release billions of spores that create clouds. These sporulated clouds, in turn, drop rain down into these environments, creating the perfect mushroom conditions. Whole tropical ecosystems are intimately coordinated by these invisible swarms of spores.

Given these facts, we can surmise that as we degrade soil and destroy underground mycelial communities, we are not only harming the ground, we are harming the sky. The source of rain isn't always above our heads. Sometimes it comes from below our feet.

Imagine, then, the small hand-sized cloud Elijah saw as a shimmering symphony of billions of spores, each nestled within a skin of water. What if the storm god Yahweh wasn't singular but scintillating with multiplicity?

How can a monotheistic sky god rule the dirt, the fungi, the funky and sexy reality of embodied life if he is always hovering above it? How can he understand the millions of different stories that constitute an ecosystem if he insists there is only one story and one god?

Monotheism is trapped by its attachment to a mythic monologue. Sky gods think sunshine, abstraction, and ascension are the answer to everything. But the problem with the sun is that if it isn't tempered by darkness and rain and decay, it tends to create deserts instead of biodiverse ecosystems. We are ground people who have been worshipping sky stories not properly suited to our relational existence rooted in the land. Sporulated storm gods come from the ground, like us, so they understand our soil-fed, rain-sweetened existence. They bring the wisdom of the underworld and lift it into the sky, only to pour it back into the leaves, the grasses, the valleys, soaking back into the dirt from which they originally emerged. Sky gods encourage linear thinking. Spore gods teach us that everything is cyclical. Yes, sometimes we must ascend like a spore on the wind, but it is also important to descend back into our bodies and back into the earth.

I return again to one of the oldest storm gods, Indra, god of rain, who is referred to as *maalai venkudai mannavan,* god of the pearl garland and white umbrella, in the oldest Hindu-Jain Tamil epic *Silappatikaram.* Indra's pearl garland is also famously known as Indra's net, a vast interconnected system of pearls or gems that hangs in the sky, each individual gem refracting back an entire world. Quantum physics has claimed the net as an example of quantum interactions. It has also been used to explain consciousness by thinkers such as Rajiv Malhotra.[4] What if Indra's net were a winking, glittering collection of spores, each attracting a water droplet and coalescing into a life-giving rain cloud? How fitting then that Indra should also arrive with his white umbrella—the umbrella cap of a mushroom, parachuting out to release spores, seed clouds, and quietly disrupt the idea of monotheism.

2

The Hanged Man Is the Rooted One

Thinking from the Feet

Every time we exalt in the verdant intelligence of a forest, we know where it keeps its brain: its roots. Right below our own feet. The root brain, poured through the soil, is less a bounded object and more a verb, encompassing and connecting a whole forest of perspectives.[1] Mycorrhizal systems represent neural diversity and biodiversity. Hyphal tips slip into and include tree thoughts, plant thoughts, bacteria thoughts, soil thoughts, and even insect thoughts.

If we get low to the ground and smell the dirt, we are aware that we are no witness. We are a participant, a node of cognition, in this great brain. Spores and dust and soil microbiome flood into our nostrils, and then we pour ourselves, our breath, back into the forest air, back into the open stomata of the trees' leaves. There is no abstraction and no disembodiment. Everything is anchored, intimately, lovingly, to matter.

Tarot, for me, is only useful as a tool insofar as it relates to my body and the landscape. The more rooted I can make the tarot's symbols, the more useful they are for bringing me into dynamic, compassionate participation with the world around me. One of the best examples is the Major Arcana card known as the Hanged Man.

Traditionally, the Hanged Man represents a pause, perhaps tinged with discomfort, that holds the possibility of enlightenment. With a corona of gold light blooming from his head, the figure calmly holds the inverted position, tied by one foot to a tree that some have posited represents Yggdrasil, the world tree of Norse mythology. Could he represent the Norse god Odin, tied to a tree for nine days so that he could receive higher knowledge and the ability to use the sacred runes? Yes. But is there an interpretation that does not evaporate into another culture's cosmologies? How can the Hanged Man help us enter more fully into our aliveness?

The Hanged Man, for me, is the Rooted One. He represents more than a physical inversion. The Rooted One initiates a perspectival shift. We blink, and suddenly the ground becomes the sky. The brain is not abstracted in the head. It lives in and is constituted by the roots. The wisdom of the Rooted One is to relax our ideas about dominant epistemological paradigms, to relax our ideas about how knowledge arrives.

First, the Rooted One shows us how to let personal, somatic understanding sink down into the soil of ourselves. Our bodies are deeply intelligent. They hold emotions. They register and respond to danger. They regulate and stimulate our breath, our appetites, our desires. They dance and flow and merge and create. How can we honor body's wisdom? In a culture that encourages us to ignore our personal sleep schedules, our aches and pains, our true hungers, our bodies' rhythms, it is important to reconnect to this type of knowledge. Our bodies, when we get to know them intimately, have a lot to tell us about what kind of medicine and movement might really benefit us.

But the Rooted One's wisdom is deeper than just the somatic. As we sink down deeper into the actual roots of plants and trees and mycelium, below our feet, the Rooted One says that there is no need to travel or seek other cultures' spiritual practices. Everything we need is right here.

Literally, right here, in the patch of dirt under our two feet.

Mycologist Paul Stamets explains that a single cubic inch of topsoil includes up to eight miles of fungal cells. By that measure he proposes that one footstep impacts three hundred miles of mycelium. The Hanged Man realizes he does not have to travel to gain understanding. His goal is to receive the specific, rooted wisdom of the landscape where he lives, eats, breathes, and loves. He doesn't even have to go on a hike or a run. One footstep reverberates through the soil, sending and receiving messages through hundreds of miles of roots.

The Rooted One wants us to understand the patch of land we call home. Each person exists inside a different landscape, a different flavor of available magic. Our greatest spiritual teacher does not need to be bought or sought. It is right where we are. It is the specific dirt between our toes. The Rooted One lets our perspective flip, so that the wisdom of the Animate Everything flows down from the feet.

When I think of what I believe in, it is closest to a form of animism—the belief that all plants, creatures, and parts of the earth are animate and alive. But it is an animism of chaotic difference. Of woven contamination. It is an understanding that my being alive does not mean I should assume that the aliveness of the hill or the river or the wild roses is the same flavor as my aliveness. Knowing that a stone is alive keeps me alive. And knowing that a stone is alive differently than me keeps me asking questions, keeps me humble and curious and open to surprise. This is the Animate Everything. The differences that sting and prick and destroy and generate and sometimes weave together to create a dense, polluted, gorgeous periwinkle sky.

The Rooted One asks, what if our brain isn't in our head? What if it is in our feet? What if it isn't even in our body? What if it is in the soil?

3

Between Naming and the Unknown

Shakespeare's Twelfth Night

In 1602 William Shakespeare debuted his play *Twelfth Night,* a gender-bending comedy whose title refers to the celebration of Twelfth Night, which takes place on the eve of Epiphany twelve nights after Christmas. Presided over by a so-called lord of misrule, the Twelfth Night celebration was characterized by its inversion of social order and Bacchic revelry.

In the play, the main character strides onto the stage. A lord of misrule? Or a lady? The player's form is slender. Elegant. Androgynous. "I am all the daughters of my father's house, and all the brothers too," the youth declares.

In Elizabethan England, all the roles would have been played by boys and men. Picture our protagonist: a boy, covered in makeup, playing the role of a youthful woman, impersonating a young man, who looks like her male twin . . . It is a thick layering of identity, gender performances, and theatrical costuming. By the end of the performance, we observe a being who practically scintillates with complex sexuality, but who, importantly, cannot and will not be named.

In fact, many readers of the play do not notice that the main character is *not* named until the final scene of the play, when she finally identifies herself as Viola. And for good reason. "Naming love too early is a beautiful but harrowing human difficulty," writes the poet David Whyte in his book *Consolations.* "Most of our heartbreak comes from attempting to name who or what we love and the way we love, too early in the vulnerable journey of discovery."

In the story of Genesis, as Adam names the animals, he finds each being useful, not in and of itself, but in relationship to his world building, his appetites, and his vocation as God's creative emissary. The creation of Genesis itself was a covert attempt by a new priestly class to prove the Jewish people's right of origin, establish a new temple, concretize a code of law, and defend the right of the Jews to the land of Judea.[1] By ascribing to Adam the "naming" of their primeval parents and the nature of creation, these people claimed ownership of a specific ecology. When Adam names the animals, he initiates an Edenic taxonomy:

> Out of the ground the Lord God formed every beast of the field, and every fowl of the air; and brought them unto Adam to see what he would call them: and whatsoever Adam called every living creature, that was the name thereof. The man gave names to all cattle, and to the fowl of the air, and to every beast of the field (Genesis 2:19–20).

Adam's final act of naming is to name his wife, Eve, inaugurating the religious basis for the masculine's ownership over the feminine. What we name, we often feel we own. What we name, we feel we understand well enough to name. And when we believe we have arrived at understanding, we stop asking questions. We close ourselves off from surprise.

Naming can easily be used as a tool of oppression. Invading the Americas, European missionaries and conquistadores erased whole peoples and languages, forcing the surviving populations to adopt Christianized names and a new language, simultaneously disappearing and reinforcing their trauma. When Europeans went on to enslave Indigenous and African people for their colonies in the Americas, they gave them new names, part of an effort to erase their identities.

Naming is often wedded to resource extraction. We name both the ecosystems we want to save and the terrains we want to demolish. The naming denotes differences in utility. The preservation of rain forests, for example, is often classified as important only when those rain forests and the biodiversity they shelter are presented as "standing reserves" of medicines, foods, and resources for our use. The construction of gender, as nested within the new global technocratic state and late-stage capitalism, is a type of naming as control, classifying us at birth. No wonder claiming a new name, never mind nonbinary pronouns, is often experienced as freedom. We escape the imposed names and strictures of our parents, our institutions, our cultural oppressions, by attempting to "own" ourselves with the magic of a self-generated nominal.

In *Twelfth Night* Viola will not name—or gender—herself too early. She understands that her role is to refuse definition. To serve as something more important than a fixed role. Upon disguising herself as a man and becoming a servant to Duke Orsino, Viola offers her service as a messenger between him and the ambivalent source of his affection, Lady Olivia. When Olivia first asks the disguised Viola her name, Viola responds easily, "I am the messenger," alluding perhaps to the word's most ancient meaning: angel. Both the ancient Greek and Middle English words for angel, *angelos* and *aerendgast,* are interchangeable as words for messenger. From this perspective Viola is the sacred intermediary. Just as angels were originally considered hermaphroditic, so is Viola, flickering like a gender palimpsest.

Both Duke Orsino and Lady Olivia fall in love with Viola, the interlocutor between nodes of gender expression, rather than with each other, the fixed signs of gender on either side of the false binary. Viola is the nexus of desire. The sacred overlap. The messenger between genders, and also the very real body of gender's indeterminacy—its constant flow between masculine and feminine.

This relationship between the hermaphroditic angel/messenger and Duke Orsino seems to be fertile terrain for a new type of masculinity. How can men learn from women to access the feminine within themselves? How can honoring our "both-ness" change courtship into a terrain that is more egalitarian, playful, and reciprocal than the patriarchal modes of romance that seem to invite sexual violence and domination? How can we honor the Viola that flickers between us and each of our lovers? The angel of our fusing desires? The place where our genders exchange nuclei and melt into a festival worthy of a lord of misrule?

Am I a man? A woman? Both? Let us wait before we answer. Answers tend to end stories. What if, like Viola, we lived the question? Let us declare a Twelfth Night celebration where we all, briefly, shed our names. Perhaps, freed of the stories we thought we were bound by, we will stumble on more fertile narratives about what it means to embody the masculine.

4

The Minotaur Dances the Masculine Back into the Milky Way

Myths Need to Move

Pasiphae had intercourse with the bull and gave birth to the Minotaur, famed in the myth. This creature, they say, was of double form, the upper parts of the body as far as the shoulders being those of a bull and the remaining parts those of a man. As a place in which to keep this monstrous thing Daedalus, the story goes, built a labyrinth, the passage-ways of which were so winding that those unfamiliar with them had difficulty in making their way out; in this labyrinth the Minotaur was maintained and here it devoured the seven youths and seven maidens which were sent to it from Athens.

DIODORUS SICULUS, *LIBRARY OF HISTORY* 4.77.1

The story goes that King Minos of Crete disobeyed the gods by refusing to sacrifice a sacred bull. In retribution the god Poseidon caused

Minos's wife, Pasiphae, to become enamored of the bull, and she then copulated with it, producing a monstrous horned child. Little is said of the Minotaur's misdoings, but he is nevertheless deemed dangerous, or at least hideous enough, that he must be sequestered away in a labyrinth that can be neither easily navigated nor exited.

Young Theseus of Athens comes to the rescue, wooing the Minotaur's sister, Ariadne, so that she reveals the secrets of the labyrinth. The patriarchal hero slays the Minotaur, wins the heart of the Cretan princess, and sets sail for more adventures, discarding Ariadne on another island almost as quickly as he had claimed her.

Theseus sets the template for heroic action: the knight or warrior who slays the dragon, the monster, the Gorgon. The hero contextualizes his valor, his purpose, by pushing against and defeating the adversary. But who is the adversary? Is it really a monster? What if I told you there was a secret inside every dragon-slaying, beast-destroying myth you've ever heard? And what if that secret was both tender and tragic? What if behind every famous monster there was a mother? When I say "mother," I do not literally mean a singular human mother or even a female. Mother indicates a matriarchal, nature-based cosmology. An earth-reverent, land-based way of being that is murdered and subsumed into a "solarized" sun god pantheon.

Let us start with the basics. "And the earth was without form, and void; and darkness was upon the face of the deep. And the Spirit of God moved upon the face of the waters," begins Genesis, a text scholars agree was probably compiled during the Babylonian exile and influenced by the surrounding Sumerian mythologies. In the Hebrew Bible, *deep*— from "the face of the deep"—is *Tehom*. As scholar A. E. Whatham points out, for Babylonian captives, Tehom would have had a very different resonance than just "deep." They would have known that Tehom of Genesis is directly tied to Tiamat, the mother sea goddess of Babylonian creation myths.[1]

In her earliest incarnations Tiamat was revered as a symbol of the primordial sea that gave rise to all of creation. However, though Babylonian religion is on a rhizomatic continuity with Sumerian religion, the acts of translation between the cosmologies were not peaceful. Tiamat came to be seen as a giant, menacing snake or dragon. She serves as one of the most painful and clearest examples of a mother transformed into a monster, narratively justifying her murder.

The transformation of Bronze Age mother-goddess cultures, or partnership societies, as Riane Eisler calls them in *The Chalice and the Blade,* began with the violent influx of Indo-Germanic tribes into the Mediterranean, decimating existing populations. Joseph Campbell, among others, characterized the resulting cultural shift as a subjugation of lunar goddess devotion by solarized hero worship.[2] In other words, nature reverence turned into nature domination.

The most well-known myth about Tiamat, the *Enuma Elish,* characterizes the mother sea goddess as hideous. She has a tail. Udders. She is huge. She is dangerously powerful. Her grandson, Marduk, called the "solar calf," is envious of her power, fears her ability to give birth to inhuman deities and monsters, and destroys her in the most obscene way possible, exploding her body, ripping her apart. The Babylonian images of this battle that survive show the direct line between Marduk slaying Tiamat and the later legends of Saint George and the dragon. In similar fashion, the earlier mother religions of the underworld goddess Inanna, the sea goddess Nammu, and the other Neolithic madonnas of vegetal regeneration and birth sink into the water below the glaring solar eye of the new sky gods and their pantheon of heroes.

The mythology of the sacred bull and the labyrinth far predate Greek myths. According to the research of acclaimed mythologist Carl Kerényi and writings of scholar Anne Baring, these stories go back to the Neolithic pre-palatial period of Crete (7000 to 1900 BCE), before the Greek invasion and fall of Minoan culture in 1775 BCE.[3]

I'll offer that the mythology of sacred bulls is even older than that. Images of bulls can be seen in the twenty-thousand-year-old cave paintings in Lascaux, France. From 4000 to 3500 BCE, as Joseph Campbell charts in his book *Occidental Mythology,* cattle cults swept across Mesopotamia, creating what he asserts is a dominant pre-Homeric, pre-Olympic pantheon of lunar bull gods and underworld goddesses. Ceremonial horns and bull heads have been unearthed in many Neolithic and early Bronze Age settlements, including the proto-cities Çatalhöyük and Harappa. More recently, the Egyptians worshipped a bull version of the god Osiris, called Apis, and also revered sacred horns and bull heads.

When we look at Greek myths—chock-full of monsters, rape, pillage, and heroic valor—we have to remember that many of these myths are translations of older stories, or at least fusions of two competing mythologies: one focused on nature reverence and mother goddesses, and the other characterized by violent heroes and a "solarization" of gods and sacred symbols. The lunar realm of the labyrinth lies, palimpsest-like, under the sunlit girth of Mount Olympus, flickering in and out of the Greek pantheon. It didn't disappear when the Indo-Germanic tribes subjugated the earlier Mediterranean populations. But, deracinated and replanted into a new, violent mythological ecosystem, earlier gods became murderous monsters, and goddesses withered into helpless princesses.

Let us look again at the Minotaur myth. And let us look closely at what archaeologists and historians have managed to reconstruct about life on Crete, a culture that Riane Eisler asserts was the healthy precursor to patriarchy. "One of the most striking things about Neolithic art is what it does *not* depict," she observes. "For what a people do not depict in their art can tell us as much about them as what they do."[4] Prior to the fall of Minoan culture, Crete had no fortified walls. Most importantly, there are no known depictions of violence or war in its extensive offering of art.

Instead, nature in all its wild fecundity is depicted in frescoes, mosaics, drinking vessels, statues, and seals. Spirals, snake-evocative chevrons, vegetation, and animals dominate the imagery. Women conduct rituals bare-breasted. Goddesses are flanked by lions. The few times that men appear, they are shown most often in positions suggesting awe and reverence, lifting their arms to a goddess or animal. Death is not depicted; neither is suffering. Physical pleasure, bulls, lunar reverence, communion with nature, and feminine divinity are prevalent. But I sense that the dominant theme here is not an object but the fluid connectivity between these symbols. Minoan culture—the origin of the Minotaur—is characterized by movement, by dance itself.

Cretan scholar Nikolaos Platon, in his *Guide to the Archaeological Museum of Heraclion,* muses about Minoan culture: "Motion is its ruling characteristic; the figures move with lovely grace, the decorative designs whirl and turn, and even the architectural composition is allied to incessant movement become multiform and complex." Nowhere is this better displayed than in the many images of the "bull dance," in which young Cretan women and men appear to leap and play with bulls. Some have speculated that this is part of a ritual sacrifice, ending with the slaying of the bull as a surrogate for a lunar king. Others postulate that the dancers themselves were the sacrifice, gored by the bull's lethal horns. But nowhere in the imagery is there blood or death. What we have is dance. Cretan culture is essentially kinetic. Divinity is reached not through heroic individualism but through connective, dynamic play. God does not dwell in the leaping youth or the charging bull but is constituted interstitially between the moving figures. The dance itself is the divine.

The Minotaur, then, is a dancer. His horns, like those of the sacred bull, echoed the shape of the crescent moon and the lunar rhythms that welcome both light and dark. The Minotaur was the god of mutability and movement. He represented the fluid, pleasureful interface between human beings and the animate world of everything else.

When Theseus slays the Minotaur, he is not slaying a monster. He is slaying an entire culture—a Cretan culture dominated by the image of a feminine divinity, flanked by lions and bulls, celebrating epiphanic communion with the natural world.

In the same way, Apollo, god of order and sterility and reason, god of the left brain, kills Python, the serpent who presided over the Oracle at Delphi, son of the mother earth goddess Gaia. Snakes are traditionally symbols of the goddess.[5] They are literally close to the earth, pressing their whole kinetic, shivering life force against her. In mythology we can see the slaying or denigration of a snake as a nod to the destruction of partnership societies, nature worship, and goddess devotion.

Perseus likewise kills the snake goddess Medusa. Both Robert Graves and Joseph Campbell thought it was quite likely that the Perseus legend references the thirteenth-century BCE invasion of the Hellenes (Aryans/Greeks), who overran the goddess's chief shrines in the Mediterranean Basin.[6]

The myth of Saint George slaying the dragon is a direct overlay of Christianity's thousands-of-years-long attempt to erase animist pagan European traditions. Who is the dragon? It could be Ireland's Cailleach or Morrigan. It could be the millions of women, femmes, and queer people who were murdered during the Inquisition for their pagan spiritual practices.

Who is the monster of today's legends? Today, we see a surfeit of media coverage devoted to weather and climate events. Has the biosphere become the monster? Every attempt to create weather- or climate-regulating technology, rather than adjusting and halting our own abysmal behaviors, posits Earth as a monster and humankind as the "heroes" who must control her and tame her and save her. Technonarcissists are the new Marduk. The new Theseus. They want the myth of progress to subsume the older (although newly investigated in the realms of quantum physics and glacial ice coring) chaos of emergent systems and biospheric intelligence. Earth doesn't know best, our cultures insist. We know best. And we must progress ever onward toward greater control.

Before his Greek bastardization into an anonymous monster, the Minotaur had a name: Asterion, or "starry one." His name may have referred to the constellation Taurus or to the rising of Sirius, an event that is correlated to Cretan festivals and sacred mead making.[7] So when we think of the Minotaur in the labyrinth, perhaps we are really seeing a solar system. The Minotaur is the guiding star. The labyrinth's winding courses are the paths of planets, objects, beings, galactic dust, caught in the divine pull of a horned nucleus.

And every star must have its Ariadne, whom we can resurrect from her defeated position in Theseus's mythology. The Linear B tablets found at the Cretan palace of Knossos read, ". . . and for the lady of the labyrinth, a jar of honey."[8] This offering shows us that the lady associated with the labyrinth is sacred, honored by a gift of wild sweetness. In *The Myth of the Goddess,* Anne Baring and Jules Cashford point out the preponderance of bulls in the myth: Passiphae's bull, the Minotaur, the bull-associated god Poseidon, and finally the savior of Ariadne, the horned bull god Dionysus, who rescues her from exile on the island of Naxos. Reading the images, we can consolidate all the bulls into one nucleus at the center of the labyrinth. The Minotaur is no longer the betrayed brother of Ariadne. He is Asterion, her partner in sacred movement: that of the swarming bees in the hive, dancing while they make Ariadne's ritual honey, and that of the dance of the bull with his human partners, leaping and rolling and charging.

Despite the preponderance of labyrinth myths and images, no remains of a labyrinth have ever been located in Crete. I want to offer another interpretation: The labyrinth was never a static object or a place. It was never a stone corridor. Instead, it was an event. It was a ritual dance to honor the bull and the annual rising of certain constellations. Each "passageway" was a chain of human hands, a serpentine gyration of gestures. The labyrinth was only ever the sacred relationship between people dancing—ecstatically, kinetically—inscribing the patterns of the sky into the soft dirt of the ground.

If the Minotaur offers the masculine anything, it is the healing power of playful, expressive movement. The kind of movement that understands it is always in dialogue with other animals, the weather, the texture and slope of the landscape between our toes. Let the masculine learn how to dance again. And like the starry Asterion, the more we dance, the more people will be attracted into our orbit of participatory, exultant celebration.

Finally, let the Minotaur stand as a reminder: There are no monsters. Only bad rewrites of forgotten stories.

5

The Moon Belongs to Everyone

Lunar Medicine for the Masculine

Masculinity is lunar. Gender is lunar. Sexuality is lunar. Landscape is lunar. Bodies, liquid in a flesh silhouette, are tides of lunacy, constantly shifting their internal shorelines. To be lunar means to change—to be full and ripe one night, and tired and reclusive another.

What is the masculine? The masculine doesn't belong to a specific type of body. The masculine, like the moon, is mutable. There is no final destination for masculinity. It flickers. Thickens. Breaks. Flows. It anastomoses, mycelial hypha by hypha, through soil. Many of the early mythological figures we have "re-rooted" are lunar. They are connected to the night, the earth goddess, the bull, and the underworld. Like plants, they are always specific flowerings suited to their environments. But once they fruit, mushrooms sporulate, sending their tiny spores on the wind to repopulate the soil of somewhere else. Why not hop a ride on one of these mythic spores and ride it to a mythological being untethered to a specific place or language? A being that we can all access, every night, from any location.

Patriarchal masculinity is painfully static. Think of the collective cultural shock when a male celebrity wears a dress to an awards show.

Men are limited, not only narratively, but visually, given shirts and pants and expected to progress, step by step, into increasingly calcified stories of achievement and strength. This isn't a gender expression. Expression implies movement and creativity. Patriarchal masculinity stays the same, and it stays still.

As climate change intensifies the likelihood of unpredictable environmental events, flexibility is key. This is best demonstrated by the idea of resilience ecology, developed by ethnobotanist Enrique Salmón. Resilience ecology is a way of describing nonlinear dynamics in ecosystems. Put simply, any type of ecosystem is resilient only insofar as it can adapt to and reshape itself as a result of shocks to its system. We are entering into an age of shocks, as the last several years of a pandemic, wildfires, and hurricanes have shown us. Organisms already know they must stay light; they know they must stay changeful.

Biology shows us that nature knows how to stay adaptable. Our very cells are the result of collaborative changefulness. Salamanders and mushrooms can both adapt their sexes in relationship to shifting environmental pressures. Sexual expression, for many beings, is ecologically flexible. *Saccharomyces cerevisiae,* a yeast used in winemaking, also has the ability to switch between sexes. The moon is a medicine that can help us practice a similar flexibility. By acknowledging our lunar ability to shift and cycle, we can prepare for an uncertain future by monthly, "moonly," developing a new mythic musculature.

People with wombs have always known that bodies and consciousness are cyclical, tied to a rhythm that is larger than the individual. The cycle is twenty-eight days, full moon to full moon. *Moon* sounds like a name or a noun. But let us remember that *moon* is a gerund. Always moving. Always moon-ing. It is time to give the masculine back its lunar knowledge. Wombs swell, yearn, mulch, and release in twenty-eight days. But a womb is not just an organ. It is an invitation that anyone of any physicality and any gender expression can accept. It is an invitation to dance inside change for twenty-eight days. To practice softness for a cycle. The masculine has a womb, too. A moon. All it need do is look up at the night sky.

What is lunar wisdom? Even on a new moon night, the moon is still present: replete and whole, while also void and occluded. This is a completion that holds loss tenderly inside its body. It is neatly summed up by Octavia Butler's powerful words: "God is change."[1] The moon is every gender, every sexuality, mostly both, always trans: waxing and waning. The moon only ever flirts with fullness or emptiness for a brief, tenuous moment before slipping into change. Here is our blended, androgynous Dionysus. Wine-drunk, love-swollen, wind-swept, in ecstatic union with the holy, the moon encourages us to dissolve our edges rather than affirm them.

Lunar knowledge keeps us limber. Keeps us resilient. Awe, whether somatic or spiritual, transforms us.

The alternative to patriarchy and sky gods is not equal and opposite. It is not a patriarchy with a woman seated on a throne. The Sacred Masculine isn't a horned warrior bowing down to his impassive empress. The divine, although it includes us, is mostly inhuman. Mutable. Mostly green. Often microscopic. And it is everything in between. Interstitial and relational. The light and the dark. Moonlight on moving water. The lunar bowl where we all mix and love and change.

6

Becoming a Home

The Empress Card Embraces the Masculine

In the tarot, the Empress card is melted butter, honeycomb, refulgent pulse of a full moon reflected in lake water. It is hard to tell where the Empress ends and the scenery begins. A stream flows into her robe, which is emblazoned with pomegranates, the symbol of Persephone and the underworld. Resting as if weightless on her flaxen hair is a crown of twelve stars, symbolizing the number of months in a year and the planets. Star and soil. Water and fruit. Wheat dances, tickling her toes. Trees encircle her resplendent throne. Her hand grasps a scepter. The sign of Venus glows in the corner, reminding us that beauty is holy, love is ritual, and fertility is a relationship between our bodies and the earth. Her lap is wide and spacious, inviting a lover or a child to climb onto it.[1]

And that is what the Empress card most represents to me: a welcoming lap, a hearth, a home. A field of blue bonnets and wild lupine, where you will unfurl your picnic blanket and set up a lunch to share with friends and whatever fairies, birds, or bees decide to join. She is the host *and* the home of the host. The table set with wine and fresh peonies. Friends, rosy cheeked, sharing stories, with their elbows accidentally resting in the soup dish. The door is open and inviting. The fire lit and the corners clean. Dried yarrow and mugwort hang from the rafters.

Hundreds of years of simplistic binaries have led us to believe that the hearth fire is tended by the feminine, while the hunt or external world is governed by the masculine. The man is welcomed back into the home, fed, and cared for, but he is never the lap of plenty. He rules the home. But he is not allowed to "be" the home.

Male chefs exist now in the realm of celebrity, treating food as if it were another country to exploit and master. Men own fashion companies and real estate. They own homes. But what does it mean to *embody* a home? To become that sacred space that calls in community and conversation and family? How often do we see the masculine as a freshly cleaned kitchen with a bowl of strawberries and whipped cream on the windowsill? A wide expanse of untilled land, gone to seed, humming with native wildflowers and pollinators?

We are all increasingly strangers in the home of our own bodies: taught to ignore our subtle appetites and changing needs, taught to medicate symptoms rather than curiously inquiring into root causes. We blast our microbiomes with antibiotics and spray away the natural pheromones that once carefully attuned us to choosing the right sexual mates. People with wombs are told that their menstruation needs to be treated with medication as if it were a disease. Food is seen as fuel, not sacrament. We treat our bodies like vehicles we can drive into the ground and then replace. We work hard to abstract our minds from our most sacred physical hearths.

The Empress card is a velvety patch of moss. A cozy armchair. She asks, "Is your body a soft place to land? Do you open the door to your own heart and breathe a sigh of relief, diving into the comfort of your own desire and sense of beauty?"

There is a wonderful natural metaphor for the Empress: the purple pitcher plant. The plant is not immediately inviting. Her magenta leaves curl to form vertical tubes, looking less like a flower and more like an exposed organ. This bromeliad is one of the infamous carnivorous plants that has developed to capture and digest insects and creepy crawlers. But there is something unique about the purple pitcher plant. When she is young and needs sustenance, her tubes capture and digest all manner of beings. As she grows hardier, her digestive enzymes weaken and the inside of her tubular leaves undergoes a dramatic transformation. The pitcher plant now becomes a home to a variety of symbiotic dipteran larvae, algae, bacteria, mites, fungi, and protists. These populations are called *inquiline communities,* meaning that they make their home from another home. They nourish the pitcher plant with their refuse.[2]

In its maturity the pitcher plant becomes more than just a plant. It becomes a nourishing, welcome place for a diversity of beings. I see a table set with food where representatives from different species come to relax and share stories from their distinct mythologies. The pitcher plant is the welcoming, candlelit space where opposing narratives and ideas meet and merge and start understanding how to live together.

What would it look like to become a welcoming home? A place where different stories and beliefs and beings could potluck and laugh and share? What would it look like to come home to ourselves? To buy flowers to place on the table of our own desires? To tend to the body as if it were a room that needed to be cleaned, its windows opened to the linden-scented spring air?

The Empress card invites in the masculine. We do not have to rule the home. We can relax and become the home. The more sacred we make our spaces, the more magic we feel called to create inside these spaces. I ask you to carefully attend to your own body as a place of refuge and community. The more fertile we let ourselves be, the more we have to share with others. As the pitcher plant grows up, it is increasingly able to welcome other beings and stories into its own body.

Let us all nourish our bodies, our dreams, our hearts, so that we can become a lap for those who need a soft place to rest. Let the Empress card turn us into the field where wildflowers, bears, blackbirds, sunshine, mushrooms, monsoon rain, and moonlight all meet to break bread.

7

Dionysus

Girl-Faced God of the Swarm, the Hive, the Vine, and the Emergent Mind

Behold, God's Son is come unto this land.

EURIPIDES, *THE BACCHAE*

Although Thebes is often identified as Dionysus's birthplace, the god of the vine's return to his land of origin is still experienced as the arrival of a stranger. Dionysus is repeatedly called the "foreign" god. The Greeks, who are often incorrectly identified as the original worshippers of the wine deity, did not, in fact, think of Dionysus as beginning within their pantheon. He was always arriving from across the sea, from another strange land. Who was this fresh-faced, long-haired young man, dressed in women's clothing with the power to transform men into grapevines, women into ravenous, predatory leopards, and water into wine?

Dionysus is a bull god. A grape god. A leopard god. The god of women. The god of androgyny and play. The god of ivy and invasive species.[1] The Orphic hymns, a collection of Greek poems dated to roughly between the sixth and fourth centuries BCE, take special pleasure in accumulating epithets and names for Dionysus rather than committing to just one. See, for example, "Orphic Hymn 30 to Dionysus" from Otto Kern's 1922 *Orphicorum Fragmenta:*

> *I call Diónysos the loud-roarer! Who wails in revel!*
> *First-Born, two-natured, thrice-born, Vakkhic king,*
> *Wild, inscrutable, cryptic, two-horned, two-shaped,*
> *Bedecked in ivy, bull-faced, war-like, howling, holy,*
> *Divine victim, feasted every other year, adorned with*
>   *grapes, bedecked in foliage.*
> *Evvouléfs, counselor, Zefs and Kóri bore you . . .*
> *on a secret bed, immortal Daimôn;*
> *Listen happy one to my voice, sweet and gentle divine*
>   *inspiration,*
> *Having a kindly heart, with the aid of your chaste*
>   *nurses!*

He is born three times. He is firstborn. He is various. And the Dionysian myths that survive accentuate this slipperiness. Dionysus disrupts our desire for a discrete, individual narrative that follows that arrow of time forward. He is immediately mycelial in his birth stories, branching off in many different directions from a variety of parents and locations.

One popular version begins with the god Zeus seducing the human princess Semele, daughter to Cadmus, an ancient Greek hero and founder of the city of Thebes. But Semele is not a Greek name. Historian Marija Gimbutas, among others, postulates that Semele represents a form of Semla, a much earlier Phrygian earth goddess mentioned by Homer, Euripides, and Ovid. Dionysus and his mother, then, can be connected to the Phrygian populations that existed before the Ionian Greek invaders came down and colonized their mythology.[2] Zeus, a new god of thunderbolts and mountain summits, copulates with an older female principle or goddess of the earth. This maps onto the Orphic cult's belief that Dionysus was born of Zeus and the earth goddess Demeter. In a particularly gruesome turn of events, Semele is destroyed mid pregnancy by the cosmic power of Zeus. Despondent, Zeus gestates the zygote Dionysus in his own thigh.

Dionysus, then, is born of man and woman. He is a blend of genders from the start, and also of elements and cultures, so it is no surprise when legends tell us he is born with bull horns or turned into a baby goat. His name dates back to as early as 1250 BCE; it is recorded in Linear B, the oldest version of Mycenaean Greek, on tablets found in Crete. But we can assume he existed even earlier than that by the recurrent themes of horns in his birth stories. He is an inheritor of the Minotaur's horns and thus connected to the narratives of the Animate Everything.

But unlike the Minotaur, Dionysus does not stay in place or a stay a bull. He is alternately "girl-faced" and "frightening" and "phrenetic" and "prudent." He is ancient, unclassifiable, and paradoxical. The only constant is Dionysus's mutability: half human, half god, he is born mid transformation, his curling tresses a swarm of snakes, horns sprouting from his head. He is raised on a mountain. In a palace. In a grove. By his aunt. By a satyr. By women. By elementals—nymphs and nature spirits and satyrs. He is raised as a goat and as a girl to protect him from Zeus's jealous wife, Hera.[3]

The important thing is that, when Dionysus arrives, it is not as Joseph Campbell's solitary hero on a quest for origins or an illusory grail. It is not even as an apocalyptic savior with a specific plan for humanity. No. Dionysus arrives grinning, virile, vegetal, embodied, with the grail already in hand. He has his kantharos (a ceremonial winged cup) filled with ferment and his flowering thyrsus (wand) conducting vegetal mayhem.[4]

Dionysus isn't on a quest. He isn't in search of anything. Instead, he travels to cities and cultures to share the sacrament he's already attained. Wine and honeyed mead. Open-air devotional dance and song. And the secrets of a Paleolithic, participatory existence with nature.

Dionysus arrives like mushrooms do after a night of rain: all at once. He is always the unexpected stranger, his flowering wand thrust into the air like a lightning rod, symbolizing his connection to his thunderbolt father. Though his celebrations become calendrical in the time of Roman rule, they were first characterized as mushroom miraculous, popping up in full swing, without any pretense or planning.

Emergent systems are characterized as systems that work as an assemblage of different entities. They represent the moment when chaos coalesces into synchronized, relational patterns of a complexity that is utterly unpredictable. Examples are the murmurations of starlings, tornadoes, and fish schooling. Dionysus never shows up alone. He always has plants, leopards, lions, women, satyrs, or goats in tow. He is covered in snakes and vines. His whole presence shimmers and flickers: between genders, between species, between new and old, between known and unknown.

Dionysus and his celebrations were akin to emergent behavior. When enough people sensed his presence, smelled mead fermenting in rainwater-flooded beehives, felt vines constricting and stroking the walls of civilized life, a type of chaotic wildness would coalesce into a new sort of group behavior. The Bacchanalian swarm. The maenads' ecstatic frenzy, when groups of women, like lion prides, hunted the hillsides for prey, working as one feline mind to seek out the ancient feast of raw meat and blood.

Dionysus, like life itself, merging and consuming and recycling matter, loves to get involved. He behaves like his symbolic vine; he twines and entangles and embraces. He is a foliage of faces, a network of connections, rather than one fixed, monotheistic identity.

Dionysus is a perfect example of a mythic mycelium. Yes, he is ancient. He runs deeper than the pantheons and cultures that celebrate him. But whenever he arrives at a new city or location, he "refruits." He adapts to circumstances, knowing that he will be most useful if he shifts his physical and spiritual form to fit the specific needs of a situated ecology and culture. Every mushroom of Dionysus is different. Perhaps, then, it is more fitting to say that he is always born, rather than his classical epithets of twice- and thrice-born. Every time his underground mycelium fruits up, he is born fresh-faced and mutable and tailored to a certain mythic emergency.

In his ability to assess and adapt to changing circumstances, Dionysus behaves like an adaptogenic mushroom. Adaptogens are curious biological mechanisms. While not completely endorsed by Western medicine (as most nonreductionist, holistic practices are not), adaptogens have been used for centuries across cultures to help bring a body or an immune system into homeostatic balance. Rather than having a specific, targeted approach to healing, adaptogenic mushrooms are dynamic and flexible. Once consumed, they perform whatever specific and individualized balancing is necessary. They adapt to the ecosystem of a human body. They are mutable, behaving intelligently in that they seem to make choices about the best approach to biological imbalances. And while these mushrooms adapt to our systems, they also teach our immune and nervous systems to be more flexible and improvisational themselves.[5]

Adaptogenic intelligence resonates with Enrique Salmón's concept of resilience ecology. Adaptogens improve a body's ability to adapt to changing conditions. An ecosystem is healthy insofar as it can adapt and come back into homeostasis. For example, the well-known mushroom reishi, or *Ganoderma lucidum,* my favorite adaptogen, stimulates the immune system and helps rejuvenate adrenals worn out from chronic overproduction of cortisol in response to stress. It is also reported, in studies with mice, to promote neurogenesis, the growth and repair of nerve tissue in the body and brain.

When we take reishi, it adapts to the needs and disruptions in our body's ecosystems. Likewise, when Dionysus arrives, he arrives flexibly, chaotically, assessing where he needs to plant his vines and nourish with fermented mead and food the disturbed narrative biome of a culture. Dionysus is not static. He is not written in stone. He flows like a fountain. He finds his shape inside the void (wound) that needs healing.

Best of all, when we work with adaptogenic heroes, letting them flow into new shapes to fit our needs—when we tell a different story about an old god—they can act like reishi in that they teach us, too, to be more flexible. They don't just improve the mythic realm. They improve the biotic, metabolic, lived experience of being in a body. They help us deal practically with the stressors of daily life.

Every day we need different routines and foods and experiences to keep our bodies fluid and nourished. Life is unpredictable. It requires improvisation. And we learn to be light on our feet by telling fluid, flexible stories. Different seasons call for different diets and movement. Different environments and soil microbiomes call up different narratives from the mycelial underworld.

Let us give back to the masculine the ability to refruit and mushroom up freshly to fit changing circumstances and evolving relationships. Let us gift them fungal flexibility to experiment with creative, spiritual, and sexual expression, knowing full well that adaptability is survival. The more the masculine can adapt, the more able it will be able to withstand strong winds and chaos. Like Dionysus, we can remember our deeper, pre-patriarchal root systems that help us stay grounded, while still able to sway in a storm. Let us give masculinity back its flowering wand of reciprocal relationship with the natural world. Let us call Dionysus to the gates of our cities and homes. A man who can dance with plants and honor beasts, a man who can be a woman and an androgen and an animal, is more than a gender. He is a celebration. A hive of humming bees. A secret network of fungus ready to erupt as the air moistens. A murmuration of birds. A cluster of grapes. A throng of singing women. A magician.

8

Merlin Makes Kin to Make Kingdoms

A Multiplicity of Minds and Myths

I put above all these things the woodland the spreading Oaks of Calidon, the high hills, the green meadows at their foot—those are for me, nor these things. Take back your goods, King Rodarch. My nut-rich forest of Calidon shall have me: I desire it above all else.

GEOFFREY OF MONMOUTH, *VITA MERLINI*

Across legends spanning all the way to the sixth century, Merlin the wizard, the famous advisor of kings, will "drop in" to teach kings, crown them, dispense poetry and wisdom, and provide distinctly animal-themed prophecy. But then, as described in Geoffrey of Monmouth's histories and the Welsh *Annales Cambriae,* he goes mad and seeks refuge in the forest.[1] When he returns to the human world, he is often wearing feathers and accompanied by a herd of stags, pigs, and wolves. Merlin teaches kings how to rule, but his teachings don't come from the world of men. They come from the kingdom of the Animate Everything itself, in all its feral, furred, fishy multiplicities.

Merlin's origin story sets up his ability to mediate between animals and men. He makes kin with other beings by literally becoming them: "I have been a blue salmon, I have been a dog, a stag, a roebuck in the mountain . . ."—the list (from thirteenth-century Wales) goes on.[2] Merlin is often equated with the bard Taliesin, and legend tells us the goddess Ceridwen turns Merlin/Taliesin into a bard by putting him through "lifetimes" as a series of plants and animals. Merlin's wisdom isn't conceptual. It is somatic. Lived. His mythology isn't calcified by a singular human perspective. In his essay "Singing with the Frogs," included in his book *Everywhere Being Is Dancing,* Robert Bringhurst recounts how the Ifugao people of northern Luzon, in the Philippines, would hold events where every priest spoke a spirit's story simultaneously—a polyphony of beings, representing intersecting, sometimes dissonant, sometimes resonant, cosmogonies. *Polyphony* is defined as independent melodies combined together to create a complex musical texture. It stands in opposition to *monophony,* where just one voice or instrument dominates, and *homophony,* where a singular musical texture is highlighted.

Ecology is polyphony. A forest of inhuman minds. Merlin knows this is where he must draw his inspiration—not from one source, but from all of them at once.

In a time of monoculture and monomythology, of tree farms and grocery-store tomatoes, it is important to understand that myths that stay the same don't survive. Or worse, they make sure *we* won't survive by reinforcing extractive behavior no longer tailored to our ecosystems. They don't adapt to changing climate and shifting social conditions. We must understand that storytelling is not a human event. It is a relationship. An ecstatic reciprocity with the Animate Everything. A relationship that is constantly changing and evolving.

That is Merlin's gift. Like the hawk that bears his name, he flies back and forth between the forest and the king's fort. He knows when he enters the trees that he is not in an inert world. He knows he is in a world of minds, and for every mind—stone mind, grass mind, lichen mind, deer mind—there is a myth, a way of making meaning. This is not a homophonic tree farm but a polyphony of beings, flying, rooting, sleeping, greening, melting, triturating down to mineral dust. In the forest there is no single myth. And, most importantly, there is no single mythology. This multiplicity of stories provides a healthy landscape, an abundantly diverse and resilient mythological biome for a kingdom.

A king is in charge of many, so he must respect and have a desire to be in relationship with many minds. As philosopher Isabelle Stengers urges, we must somehow make decisions in the presence of those who will bear their consequences.[3] Not only does Merlin understand this, his trans-species initiation has shown him that when we make decisions in the audience of other beings, we are participating in—sharing a root brain with—that aliveness. A kingdom is not a linear progression toward homogenous unity. A kingdom is a contrapuntal composite of stories, voices, melodies, plants, geologies. Merlin can't stay in the king's court for long, sharing the increasingly stale wisdom. Just as his story has been continually updated by poets and historians, scholars and authors, he keeps himself fresh by continuing to return to the forest with different questions.

But Merlin's mythic device is not the utilitarian hunt and capture of patriarchy. This is the tentative hand held out to the mourning dove. The white lace of matsutake kissing into the pine tree. Merlin keeps flexible by making kin. He understands the kingdom not by teaching kings to conquer it, but by teaching them how to come into relationship with a biodiversity of stories. His teaching is simple: When you need advice, don't always go to another human being. Go to the woods. The animals. The weather. The American chestnut, all but extinct, but somehow still standing behind your apartment. Make new kin. Tell new stories.

9

Joseph, Secret Vegetalista of Genesis

Plants Use Men to Dream

Behold, this dreamer cometh. Come now therefore, and let us slay him, and cast him into some pit, and we will say, Some evil beast hath devoured him: and we shall see what will become of his dreams.

GENESIS 37:19–20

In Genesis Joseph is the youngest and favored son of Rachel and Jacob. Like his famous father, he is prone to visions and mysticism. Unfortunately, he makes the mistake of openheartedly sharing his intuitions with his older brothers, men he considered his kin and intimate friends, but they end up throwing him into a pit and selling him into slavery. Eventually Joseph lands in Egypt, where, through his intuitive prowess, he becomes the king's vizier.[1]

Here we see a man who, like Dionysus, does not conform to rigid gender roles. Genesis tells us again and again that Joseph weeps. He dreams. He wears a brightly colored ornamental cloak. And, most damningly, he channels the dreams of plants—wheat in particular.

Joseph's superpower is his sensitivity to the vegetal imaginal realm. This is what eventually sets off his spiteful brothers: Joseph shares with them a dream in which he witnessed sheaves of wheat bowing down before him. His brothers view this dream as prideful. Who is Joseph to think he can have prophetic dreams? Who is he to think he can receive dreams from plants? Or from God?

But what if Joseph's dream had less to do with hierarchal structures and more to do with ecological initiation? What if the wheat was bowing before Joseph in his dream as a symbol of vegetal vocation? Joseph is being invited into his dreaming role as the intermediary between plants and people. In Genesis, Joseph provides a mouthpiece for the wisdom of the wheat.

Ethnobotanist and poet Dale Pendell writes about the tradition of "dreaming plants" as it still exists in South America: "Along the upper Amazon . . . there are yachaqs who learn shamanism directly from the doctores, the plant teachers. . . . These yachaqs are also called vegetalistas. Every true vegetalista has to meet . . . the Forest Person . . . face to face. In the jungle."[2]

Ethnobotanists have long wondered how Indigenous people the world over can so quickly and easily identify plant varieties that seem impossible to differentiate. Further, how did ancient peoples determine which plants were poisonous, medicinal, magical?

What if this epistemological issue is one of dreaming? What if we have forgotten how to let plants dream through us? They have plenty to share. But we keep throwing their interpreters (poets, naturalists, artists, musicians, and "others") into the symbolic pit. Their epistemological approaches don't conform to material reductionism. Where is the residue of a dream? Where is the data? The proof?

Patriarchy associates dreaming with fiction. Dreaming can't be quantified or measured with an apparatus. But dream incubation was considered to be a cutting-edge technology even well into the time of the Roman Empire. Invalids, looking for a cure, would go to sleep in the temples of Asclepius, god of healing, in order to receive curative dreams. The specific location was important. A pilgrimage to sleep in a certain place associated with a deity and receive the dreaming that fruited upward, from underground, was central to the practice. The dream came from the land.[3] Our ancestors, temporally closer to Paleolithic earth-based traditions, still understood that dreaming was a mode of divine communication.

The problem for Joseph is that the men of Genesis were already shaped by dominator culture. They were already suffering from sky god amnesia, forgetting that their agricultural knowledge and their mythological health came not from the heavens but from the underworld: lunar dreams, root systems, and mythic mycelia. Most gods have roots. And sometimes a god is a plant that uses men to dream.

Initially, Joseph runs into trouble in Egypt, where he is thrown into prison for inspiring the desire of his master's wife. But his vegetal dreams save him. A bundle of grapes, evocative of Dionysus's fermented magic, help Joseph interpret a royal cupbearer's dream. The cupbearer, impressed by Joseph's mystical skills, recommends his services to the pharaoh, who has been repeatedly plagued by dreams of hungry cows. Once again, the wheat "speaks" through Joseph, foretelling seven years of plenty followed by seven years of severe drought.

Some scholars suggest that Joseph was a historical figure, sitting right at the center of the Bronze Age collapse between 1200 and 1150 BCE.[4] Conflicting theories attribute this collapse to volcanic eruptions, the rise of phonographic scripts, and ironworking. But one thing remains constant: sweeping droughts and famine killed off huge populations. Canaan, the home of Joseph, did in fact suffer from famine. So when we read that Joseph's brothers threw him into the pit, we are seeing this new patriarchal religion throwing away its people's ability to predict, adapt to, and prepare for environmental change.

The plants were attempting to help Jacob and his sons through the dream channel of Joseph. But the men of Canaan no longer trusted plant dreams, and worse, they no longer trusted each other. Interestingly enough, once sold into slavery, Joseph finds himself in a place where Bronze Age beliefs still persist: his visionary wisdom finds recognition in Egypt, where he quickly rises in power. Joseph advises that the pharoah's dream of seven lean cows eating seven fat cows indicates that there will be seven abundant years followed by seven years of famine. The pharaoh heeds the wheat's warning, channeled through Joseph, and stockpiles grain. The Egyptians survive the famine on stored surplus.

The great wheat kernel of wisdom in this story is also its wound: everyone suffers when men doubt other men's intimate dreams. The themes of the Genesis narrative are men dreaming of plants, men trusting other men with their secret visions, and men facing violence and disbelief when they are vulnerable. What does it mean when men stop trusting plants and their own intuition? Worse, what does it mean when men stop trusting other men with their spiritual questions and visions? What would it look like for men to ask plants, fungi, flowers, and landscapes for wisdom about how to deal with the oncoming climate collapse? And how powerful would it be if our brothers didn't laugh at us? What if dreaming of plants wasn't just a passing fantasy but a mystical, masculine birthright?

10

Actaeon Is the King of the Beasts

From Curse to Crown

Without more threats, she gave the horns of a mature stag to the head she had sprinkled, lengthening his neck, making his ear-tips pointed, changing feet for hands, long legs for arms, and covering his body with a dappled hide.

OVID, *METAMORPHOSES*

The legend of Actaeon, according to Ovid, has the young Theban hunter surprising the goddess Artemis bathing. Outraged, the goddess transforms him into a stag that falls victim to his very own hunting dogs. But Ovid's version of the myth is actually a relatively late retelling. There are multiple versions of the story, with a different reason for Actaeon's transformation and death in each one. The one stable element of the story seems to be that a young hunter, upon encountering the goddess of a sacred grove, is given the horns of a stag.

In the eighth-century BCE genealogical poem the *Great Ehoiai*, we encounter the oldest version of Actaeon's downfall. Here his sin is falling in love with Semele, who will be Dionysus's mother, which provokes the jealousy of Zeus. Thus, when Actaeon is turned into a stag, it is as punishment for his love of a woman claimed by the gods. Historian Michael C. Astour has demonstrated that the story seems to have its root earlier still in the 2000 BCE *Epic of Gilgamesh*. When Ishtar, the goddess of fertility and love, tries to seduce Gilgamesh, he is wary and replies:

> *You loved the herdsman, shepherd and chief shepherd*
> *Who was always heaping up the glowing ashes for you,*
> *And cooked ewe-lambs for you every day.*
> *But you hit him and turned him into a wolf,*
> *His own herd-boys hunt him down*
> *And his dogs tear at his haunches.*[1]

Gilgamesh is already an epic informed by the extractive and domineering themes of patriarchy. The goddess, then, is always to be feared in her intimate relationship to the natural word. Her relationship to male suitors becomes an echo of humanity's relationship to environment. Here we can see the original echoes of Artemis turning her fury on Actaeon. The sacred grove of Artemis is like the sacred cedar groves of Mesopotamia cut down by Gilgamesh.

Once ecocide begins our myths contract around goddess figures; we already subconsciously fear retribution and back-form stories of the punishment we secretly anticipate. We can see, clearly, Actaeon as the receptacle for such ecological guilt in this passage. Across myths, Actaeon is not only a hunter but a shepherd, indicating that he has inherited the role of Ishtar's former lovers and other companions of the goddess, such as the shepherd Dumuzi, consort of Inanna, and Attis, always holding his shepherd's crook, consort of the goddess Cybele.[2]

Most interestingly, another figure resonates with the tragic Actaeon: the horned shepherd god Pan. Pan, like Actaeon, is also, in his earliest cults, associated with the hunt. The Greek poet Theocritus tells us that in Arcadia, when a hunt had been unsuccessful, hunters would beat statues of Pan in disappointment, asking for his divine intercession.

A man transformed into a stag. A man with horns. What if the story of Actaeon, like the myth of the Minotaur, is a translation of a Paleolithic figure into a patriarchal pantheon? Most of our information about Actaeon isn't textual but iconographic. He is painted on drinking vessels and plastered to walls. He is sculpted and carved. What speaks, then, is not the moral interpretation of the events but two images: the epiphanic moment of a young man encountering the goddess, reminiscent of the Minoan seals showing young men encountering a goddess figure on mountaintops, and the image of a man with horns.

The horned man, or the horned god, is one of the oldest visual archetypes. We see him first as "The Sorcerer" painted on the walls of Trois-Frères Cave in Ariège, France. The figure is upright, with legs and torso that suggest a man. He has an erect phallus. But his most noticeable feature is his antlers. While the mythologies of the oral cultures that left us these images persist only as oneiric flashes in more recent legends and folklore, we can still infer that the horned man was an important enough figure that he deserved to be memorialized again and again in paint and stone and, famously, on the silver Gundestrup Cauldron, unearthed from a peat bog in Denmark and dated to around 200 BCE. Here, a man is seated in a posture reminiscent of the Buddha, surrounded by animals and crowned by impressive horns. He holds a snake and a torque (metal collar), evoking dominion over both cyclical and linear time: the serpentine, forward flow and the torque's circling return. He has been identified as Cernunnos, a name attached to the horned god of the Gauls. But it may be more fitting to call him the lord of the beasts—lord of them because he is, in fact, one of them.

An interesting feature of oral, pre-patriarchal cultures is their focus on images of animals and their relative disinterest in heroic individuals and human beings. Where humans do appear, they have animal features or, most often, are faceless stick figures. The animals, on the other hand, are exquisitely fleshed out.[3] Paleolithic drawings have little need to render the divine as human. The goddess is everywhere. Every animal and plant.

Even later, in the Bronze Age, we see that Minoan culture depict bulls, snakes, bees, and natural events with much more regularity than human beings.

The Greek and Roman myths tell us Actaeon was cursed by Artemis: "Look at Actaeon's wretched fate, who by the man-eating hounds he had raised, was torn apart."[4] His own dogs are demonized and his stag form is "wretched." Inspecting the history of human culture and art, it would appear that for many thousands of years to be an animal was the highest honor of all. But by the time of Actaeon's story, animals, once divine, are now the receptacle for the anxiety produced by ecological imbalance. When we mistreat the land and overhunt animals into extinction, when like Gilgamesh we cut down the forest that houses divine beings, we fear those divine beings will retaliate.

Now that we have replanted Actaeon in a Paleolithic tradition of horned gods, I think there is something tender visible at the center of the tragic story. Something that might be helpful to resurrect.

If animals are sacred, then being turned into an animal might be considered the most magical event of all. This idea persists in Celtic and Arthurian legends. What if the goddess who turns Actaeon into a stag isn't cursing him but blessing him?

We see the goddess overlap with nature in Paleolithic artifacts and art. What if the act of turning a man into an animal was the ultimate gesture of love? What if we are really witnessing a marriage? A sacred union? To wear the horns was to be wed to the world. You could only stand beside the goddess, mate with her, run as fast as her, if you shed your human constraints. What if the horns weren't a curse but a crown?

Let us give Actaeon back his crown as lord of the beasts and king of the forest. He isn't a tragic figure. He is a forgotten king. Actaeon teaches the masculine to look closely and curiously at the places, peoples, and figures that inspire fear. What if this fear keeps us from connecting with a larger, more tender story? What are the dogs in our lives? What is the terrifying goddess?

They might just be trying to give us a gift. A wider lens. A feral mind.

11

A New Myth for Narcissus

Seeing Ourselves in the Ecosystem

Fool, why try to catch a fleeting image, in vain? What you search for is nowhere: turning away, what you love is lost! What you perceive is the shadow of reflected form: nothing of you is in it. It comes and stays with you, and leaves with you, if you can leave!

OVID, *METAMORPHOSES*

The moral tale is simple enough. A beautiful boy is born to the river god Cephissus and the nymph Liriope. The handsome youth rejects the romantic advances of both women and men. Cursed by his scorned lovers, he gazes into a pool and falls in love with his own reflection. Ovid has Narcissus die of grief and turn into a narcissus flower, while earlier myths say that he commits suicide. But the story is read as an allegory about solipsism and vanity, rather than as a tragedy.

The story has been the inspiration behind plenty of art. It has also fueled simplistic psychoanalysis and a surplus of bad literature. I'm not saying that narcissism doesn't exist. I want to offer instead that it isn't located in the watery pool or the eyes of the beautiful youth. While we are quick to chastise a teenager taking selfies, and art history loves a nude woman with a mirror as a nod to feminine vanity, we remain largely unaware that we are in love with our own moralizing. As John Berger brilliantly observes, "You painted a naked woman because you enjoyed looking at her, you put a mirror in her hand and you called the painting *Vanity,* thus morally condemning the woman whose nakedness you had depicted for your own pleasure."[1]

More recently, I have seen this narcissism inside philosophy that claims that we cannot access the real. In the Kants and Heideggers who explain that every being is withdrawn into itself. That everything we see is coated in a projection of our own worldview. While this can be a helpful reminder that our flavor of consciousness, our socialization, and our expectations influence what we see, it has also been the grounds for a new "unreality"—the idea that the real is always inaccessible, and the self is always cloaking the real.

Academia, across disciplines, has been increasingly caught in tautological investigations. Let me examine my words and find the reflection of myself inside their syntax. Let my philosophy always be a deferral of action, a dilation of the ways in which I appear in everything I study. Let me measure the placement of this electron, and find that my measurement device, my observing brain, entangles with the electron itself. Timothy Morton, a key contributor to ecological discourse and philosophy over the past decade, cuts to the core of the problem in his book *Dark Ecology,* writing, "At the very moment at which philosophy says you can't directly access the real, humans are drilling down ever deeper into it."

We have turned the world into our glassy pool. We claim natural resources as Heideggerian standing reserves, claim nothing is truly alive and bumptious and accessible, hold long meaningless debates about whether or not the world is a digital simulation. Our worldview has become Narcissus's mirror.

Perhaps the Narcissus myth resonated differently two thousand years ago. But today, simplistic interpretations of the myth seem like a misdirection. What is the beautiful youth really doing as he gazes into the watery depths of a forest pool? The overculture would have us believe he is being vain or lazy. But I'm going to attempt a new interpretation. What if Narcissus is showing us what we really need to be doing?

The glossy mirror of narcissism is the myth of progress, the flickering screens in our pockets, the idea that nothing we encounter is really real. The pool, scummed with algae, glittering with pollen, a frog eye surfacing like the visual apparatus of the water itself, is the mirror of inclusion. It doesn't show Narcissus a sterile, anthropocentric reflection. Instead, it offers something much more nutritious: the Animate Everything. The wild multiplicity of the whole world that includes us. Yes, maybe he sees his face. But it is a face rippled by a fish disturbing the silt below. It is a face turned iridescent by a dragonfly wing skimming the surface of the water.

We have no more time for abstraction. And we have no more time for moralizing. Species collapse every day, bringing down other beings they have been mutualistically involved with for millennia. But, conversely, the emergency of our situation does not call for the manic techno-narcissistic death dance of trying to "fix" the world. It calls for slowing down. For sitting next to the pool. And looking into the water.

If we are lucky, we will see ourselves.

But not as an isolated subject in the abstracted blank space of phenomenological ontology. Or in the metaverse of digital binaries. We will see that we are in the pool. We are not outside of the life forms that we are damaging and polluting. We are intimately of them. The real narcissism is to believe we can stand apart philosophically, or morally. And yes, let us, like Narcissus, fall in love with this more complex reflection. A reflection that contextualizes our being inside of, and dependent on, many other modes of being.

12

Everyone Is Orpheus

Singing for Other Species

Is he someone who dwells in this single world? No:
both realms are the source of his earthly power.
He alone has known the roots of the willow
can bend the willow-branch into a lyre.

RAINER MARIA RILKE, *THE SONNETS TO ORPHEUS*

My first encounter with the mystic musician was as metaphor, a silken strand of language linking flowers and trees to tragic love and spiritual questing. Years later, Orpheus arrived again, gently pressed between the vellum pages of the fourteenth-century Auchinleck manuscript, a compendium of popular Middle English tales. In one of the Romances, "Sir Orfeu" is a king whose queen has been stolen away, not to the underworld, but to the underground of fairy. In this version of the Orpheus narrative, the story ends happily. Sir Orfeu enchants the fairy king with his lyre playing and wins back his lady from the green world of willow roots.

Orpheus the king. Orpheus the Austrian poet Rilke's muse. When I finally investigated his origins in Rome and Greece, I wasn't surprised to discover that Orpheus had never really been a single mythological character. Aristotle and his contemporaries regarded the poems attributed to Orpheus as being authored by many different writers. Modern studies of classical texts and traditions have substantiated this perspective. Like Homer, Orpheus is plural. Rather than naming a specific heroic individual, Orpheus appears to have been used more as a spiritual title. You didn't pray to Orpheus. You prayed *as* Orpheus: through lyric and poetry and ecstatic worship of the natural world.

Orpheus mushrooms up across cities and cultures, always adapted to a particular ecosystem. The Orpheus of Thrace is different from the Orpheus of Rome. The Orpheus of Ovid belongs wholly to Ovid. This plurality resonates with the mythic bones of his story: A man journeys to the underworld and then returns. A god dies and is reborn. Every time his story is summoned, it is reborn differently.

Thinking with mycelium, we see Orpheus intimately looping with the landscape. Orpheus's dismemberment by maenads echoes other gods' mythic dismemberment, including Osiris and Dionysus. Each of these dying and resurrecting deities fruits up from a similar underground mycorrhizal system that produces gods associated with vegetation, the underworld, music, poetry, love, and springtime.

Both Anne Baring and Joseph Campbell show how these "deaths" were seen as the ferment that replenished the soil and created the healthy compost of springtime.[1] Orpheus descends to ascend, and then to die again. He stitches the world to the underworld. Mythic realm to musical reality. The link is the lyre, fashioned from that other hero of both sides: the tree, with its legs in the air and its root brain in the soil.

The honey fungus in Malheur National Forest, in Oregon, is more than 2.4 miles wide and estimated to be somewhere between two thousand and seven thousand years old.[2] Each year the invisible strands of hyphal starlight, woven below the soil, connecting tree to plant to tree, fruit upward into impressive aboveground mushrooms. Each mushroom is a poem of a certain place, an eruption suited to a specific patch of moss, distribution of sulfur, supply of sugar from symbiotic plants, and forest-floor detritus. Each mushroom is also only a small bloom of a much larger older body below the ground.[3]

I've begun to think of Orpheus's trip to the underworld as a hint at his larger mythic mycelium. He pops up as different poets and musicians and men, but he is always concerned with living in ecstatic, loving relation to the animal and plant world. His goal is not individual attainment. It is melted, porous communion with the entire forest. As Rainer Maria Rilke noted, his underworld trip has shown him that his lyre is always shaped by the rhizomatic world below.

Orpheus never grows rigid because he never stays the same. He always refruits as a different mushroom to suit the ecological, cultural, and emotional needs of a specific time and place. His multiplicity indicates his mythological health. Orpheus is flexible, mutable, adaptable.

I think Orpheus offers us (men, women, nonbinary lichenized beings that we all are) a novel opportunity. He shows us that we need not immediately speak. First, we should listen. We should listen with our feet, our ears, our minds, and our desires. In order to be an Orpheus, we must be quiet and journey to the blind, purple center of our own hearts. We each have our forest of connections that constitute our specific fruiting body. We each have our hyphal threads that connects us to a deeper mycelium of land-based wisdom.

Orpheus asks us to go outside and take off our shoes. And he asks us, what will we provide a mouth for? Each of us is invited to mushroom into our own Orpheus. What mythic mycelium twines around and into our feet? What stings our blood with an emergency of song? Will we be the Orpheus of frogs? The Carolina wren? The feeling of spring sunlight piercing through the first yellow locust leaves?

Take a moment, and if you have access to the internet, look up the last recorded song of the Kaua'i'ō'ō bird species. It is singing to a mate that will never arrive.[4] Listen to the plaintive lilt and questioning descent of the song. Attune your ear to the void space that shows you the shape of the lover that no longer sings a reply. Feel the vibration in the bones of your face, in the wave of your mind, and then, let a hunger bloom in your body for the missing song.

A bright note. A dipping stroke of melody. Something breaks through the trees and greets your ears. You feel it coil and uncoil in your own throat, begging you to respond with your own song. Is it someone playing a harp? Someone singing? No! It is a bird. The song of the Kauaʻiʻōʻō is the song of Orpheus. The soulful dirge of the lover whose Eurydice is gone and will not return. This is music that is raucous with frustration and longing, while also celebrating and delighting in the mate that no longer exists. Music that can convince the god of the underworld to relinquish the linear arrow of human time. Perhaps, like the hummingbird, we can fly backward and undo loss and pain. Perhaps, alongside Orpheus, we can even charm death and bring lost Eurydice back to life.

Interestingly, in some of the myths Orpheus does in fact succeed in saving his dead wife. What is important is not Eurydice's resurrection so much as Orpheus's ability to surrender himself to an act of grief that transforms time, opens the underworld, and finally drives other people so mad they must tear Orpheus apart and scatter his body as compost for the soil of a future springtime. His music catalyzes animal-like behavior that, ultimately, fertilizes and regenerates the land. His song serves three purposes: to celebrate what is lost, to move through mourning, and to agitate the listening audience into relational action.

When we think of Orpheus, we think of gentle harp music. I invite you now to hear the howl, the bark, the moan, the keening bird trills— the polyphony of animals surrounding their beloved musician, resonating with his bottomless grief.

Solastalgia is a new word for a new type of heartbreak. The term was coined by scholar Glenn Albrecht to describe a form of emotional distress caused by environmental change.[5] It encapsulates the homesickness for a home or a lover that no longer exists. Eurydice resonates with these lost landscapes and species. She is the green slick of melted glaciers, the old-growth forests chewed into sawdust, the crumbling coastline of Louisiana.

In her book *Staying with the Trouble,* Donna Haraway describes a bee orchid whose flower has evolved into the shape of specific female bee to attract a male bee pollinator.[6] That pollinating bee is now extinct. The flower, increasingly unable to reproduce due to its missing symbiotic partner, remains as a type of visual mourning song to the lost bee.

As more and more species disappear every day, their mutualistic relations also fray. None of us are disconnected. Each death opens up a wound—and a song. Haraway writes, "Grief is a path to understanding entangled shared living and dying; human beings must grieve *with,* because we are in and of this fabric of undoing. Without sustained remembrance, we cannot learn to live with ghosts and so cannot think." If we do not acknowledge the massive, system-wide losses that are pockmarking the landscape, we will become frozen. We will not be able to release and surrender, like Orpheus, to the song that could create new complicated connections. Haraway, influenced by anthropologists Deborah Bird and Thom van Dooren, urges us not to avoid the entangled, slow work of mourning, and insists that, in fact, grief work is necessary to sustain long-term activism.

The death of Eurydice transforms Orpheus into an underworld traveler who brings subterranean wisdom back into the daylight. But most importantly, it brings him into greater relationship with the world itself: with the texture and decay of the soil and the piercing songs of those who have also experienced transformative loss. Suddenly everything is exquisitely, painfully alive.

Orpheus is famous for having made even the stones dance with his music. The secret to this, I think, is that he knew the stones were alive. To express their aliveness, they just needed the right rhythm. His wounding opened up a space for cocreating with the Animate Everything. How can we acknowledge the lost songs that haunt our days? How can we, like the bee orchid, use our bodies and our creative outlets to memorialize, mourn, and act on behalf of our lost beloveds?

Orpheus asks men to remember to sing into the void. He asks us all to remember that if we believe the stones can dance, they *will* dance.

If we believe we can transform death and confound linear time, our belief may open unexpected doors. Orpheus asks the masculine to acknowledge all the lost songs. He asks for us to go to the bee orchid and to ask carefully and respectfully, "How can I honor the pollinators that no longer arrive?" He goes to the Kauaʻiʻōʻō bird and he bows his head, grows feathers, grows hollow bones, and sings back as the lost beloved.

Every mode of the masculine has a lyre. A mode of communication. What is yours? In an age of ecological crisis, we need poets and artists to shed the fictional constraints of sterile individuality. We need musicians to sing the song of every small being. To remind us, intimately, that every melody, although its vibrations travel the air, has emerged from the Orphic world of mycorrhizae and vegetal roots.

13

Dionysus as Liber

The Vine Is the Tool of the Oppressed

Women loved Dionysus. And he loved them. "Thus must I speak clear to save my mother's fame, and crown me here," Dionysus declares at the start of *The Bacchae*.[1] The god has returned to Thebes to honor and avenge the memory of his earth goddess mother, the Phrygian Semele. In later myths he is flanked by the dynamic mother-daughter duo of the Eleusinian mysteries: Demeter and Persephone. Dionysus is always contextualized by female lovers, mothers, sisters, and priestesses. Maidens and mothers, picking up their flowering wands, donning their animal skins, are always the first to join his sacred swarm. As soon as they fall into stride beside the leopard-pelted god, they undergo a dramatic change, shifting into the feral mindset of the maenad. The Romans, afraid of the revolutionary and unpredictable quality of this pre–Mount Olympus, open-air mystery cult, worked hard to cast the maenads in a bad light. *Maenad* derives from *manesthia,* "to rave." Dionysus's women were considered to be dangerously mad.

In a culture that was increasingly repressive of women, viewing them as untrustworthy domestic servants correctly confined to the home, what exactly *is* madness? Madness, it seems to me, would be for a woman to accept a status as second-class citizen. To accept a life without poetry, without love, and without access to wilderness—these seem much more maddening than running off to the woods to celebrate spiritual connectivity and the power of a handsome, generous, and empathic god.

What was so shocking about the maenads? Euripides describes them with long loose hair, unbound and uncovered by a veil. They tamed wild animals and wore crowns fashioned of thorns and serpents. They were draped in fawn and leopard skins, symbolic attributes of the ancient Bronze Age nature goddess Cybele, and they wielded Dionysus's fennel thyrsus. They danced and sang and ran through the groves. They drank wine and hunted wild animals with superhuman agility and strength. They ate raw flesh, a practice demonized by "civilized" Rome and then the patriarchal sterility of modern academia. But it seems obvious that this rite of flesh eating is intimately related to the leopard and feline skins the women were wearing. They were enacting rites we see in shamanic practices worldwide: becoming the animals they worshipped, inhabiting a wild mind, and participating intimately in animal appetites in order to obtain spiritual wisdom deeply rooted in their ecosystems. We delight in Ovid's palatable poetic treatments of transmogrification. What is it about the maenads' metamorphosis into lionesses that is so frightening?

Put simply, maenads are women who know they aren't different from the natural world. They are its poetic, feral creations. And thus, they are women reunited with older spiritual and ritualistic traditions that acknowledged their power. This is one of the reasons Dionysus was increasingly seen as a dangerous god by Roman authorities. It is one of the main reasons he has been discredited as a drunken fool. Dionysus is not just the god of wine. He is the god of women. He comes to honor the maidens and the mothers and to reconnect them to a mythic mycelium that predates the rise of dominating hierarchies during the Iron Age. He "crowns" them like he crowns Ariadne, returning to them their ecologically situated mystical authority that last fruited on Crete.

Dionysus, fully comfortable in a softened, feminine expression of the divine masculine, opens up a generous space for his powerful female consorts. He lets them express complexity and wildness. He gives them a freedom of expression they are denied within the bounds of a repressive culture. His is a generous magic.

Today, the feminine, like the masculine, is given a very rigid narrative of what type of physical presentation and behavior is culturally acceptable. Women are expected to starve themselves into the shape of prepubescent girls, shave their pubic and underarm hair, hide their nipples under padded bras. Paradoxically, they are expected to be highly visible and attractive on social media, while maintaining privacy, control, and physical containment. Their rage and anger is mocked, repressed, and punished. The passivity of depression and sorrow is encouraged over the dynamism of angry problem-solving.

What if the masculine could call forth and celebrate more than just the starved, porcelain maid? What if the masculine was so plural, so mutable, so relaxed and confident in its ability to flow and shift, that it opened up room for the maenad? What would it look like to allow the women in our lives to express their full complexity? I suspect the transformative alchemy of that experience wouldn't benefit only women. I think it might just have the power to turn men into gods and revolutionaries.

Dionysus was also popularly called Liber.[2] In fact, this version of the vegetal god's name is the root of our words for freedom and liberation and deliverance. Why, then, do we only think of Dionysus as a god of drunken foolishness? His worshippers very clearly saw him as a god of revolution and independence. Mythically, his arrivals signaled the inversion of social norms and the blooming of unfettered, uncivilized celebration, often conducted by a society's underdogs. This behavior isn't just fermented ecstasy. This is spontaneous, unruly revolt.

Dionysus's transformation into a red-faced wino was a deliberate smear campaign by the Romans, who saw him as a potent threat to their imperial order. Not only did he inspire women to return to older, subversive nature rituals, he inspired and incited actual revolts. Dionysus's worship wasn't only chaotic and antiauthoritarian; sometimes it was threateningly organized. Dionysus directly inspired two of the most fully realized revolts against the Roman state.

The first was the Third Servile War, led by Spartacus, an escaped Thracian gladiator, in the first century BCE. He was famously aided by his wife, a Dionysian priestess, who is reported to have gone into prophetic trances and helped the slave leaders make tactical decisions.[3] It is important to note, as well, that both Dionysus and Orpheus are said to have Thracian origins. The Thracian gladiator Spartacus was the product of a culture with a deep mythic mycelium that understood vegetal intelligence, underworld mysticism, and Dionysian liberation.

The second Dionysian revolt was led by Campanian priestess Paculla Annia. Roman historian Livy tells us that this powerful woman sought to expand celebrations of the wild god, while also opening initiation to young men. Dionysus usually had only priestesses, so this shift wasn't altogether surprising. But according to Livy—our only source on the details of her life—her critics claimed that this was a direct attempt to radicalize sons of the Roman elite so that they would turn on their fathers.[4] While the increasingly popular "cult" of Paculla Annia was never openly combative, it inspired such fear in the Roman Republic that mass trials and executions were conducted to wipe out all the followers. It is estimated that as many as seven thousand people were killed. Afterward, the worship of Dionysus was almost completely prohibited.

Let us give Dionysus back his revolutionary backbone. The god of wine and pleasure is also the god of the subversive tactics, revolution, and the oppressed. But as we recontextualize Dionysus, let us keep in mind the very important reminder from poet-philosopher Audre Lorde: "the master's tools will never dismantle the master's house."[5]

It is important to note that Spartacus fell in battle and his revolt failed. Sword hit sword. Warrior defeated warrior. In the spirit of context, Lorde was writing about Black women and Black Lesbian experiences. I am calling on her writing while acknowledging I benefited from the system that inspired its creation. I am attempting to situate myself and this writing within the entanglement of culpability. We are never wholly innocent or guilty. The master's tools will never dismantle the master's house. But what can we do if we live in the house? The master's house must be acknowledged. We cannot separate ourselves from the oppressive systems that both benefit and harm us.

Dionysus offers us a radical option. He is the god of the vine and of ivy: serpentine, tentacular vegetation that climbs, probes, constricts, and crawls. Vines and ivies are known as opportunistic plants. They twine up buildings. Inject their aerial roots into tiny cracks between bricks. Wisteria will wind around power lines, chimneys, and trellises until, anaconda-like, it overwhelms its host. Gardening and home-care manuals warn against vines damaging gutters, roofs, and windows. They digest and distend weak surfaces. Old buildings covered with ivy act as greenhouses for warmth and moisture, slowly rotting through the walls and wood behind the verdant exterior.

My favorite example in the Hudson Valley of New York, where I live, is the wild grape, whose blood-red veins finger through the foliage, circling tree trunks and corkscrewing into bushes. Its embrace is so passionate it often kills the one it embraces. What kind of a tool is that? Some bemoan the fact that the vines suffocate certain trees. My question is, are these the same trees that cannot thrive in an increasingly humid environment? Is the grapevine teaching us something subversive? An ecosystem narrative rather than a human narrative?

Simplistic environmental interpretations view invasives as detrimental. But herbalists Stephen Harrod Buhner and Timothy Lee Scott have worked to demonstrate that invasive plants like grapevine are actually just working on much larger time scales.[6] In fact, if we relax our colonized ideas about purity, we can see how invasives often arrive on the scene in order to clean up pollution, regenerate degraded soil, and offer medicine for new diseases, both parasitic and viral. The invasive knotweed, with its woody bamboo-like trunks, is a crucial herb in treating Lyme disease. Sometimes the winding vines and ivy that appear to be damaging buildings and changing the structures of our forests are actually performing a vital and uncanny act of necessary transformation.

Climate collapse will not be solved by techno-narcissism. Patriarchy will not be cured with shame and guilt. Racism cannot be cut out of our brains with a sword. Neither can we escape the system by running to the forests. The wounds of patriarchal capitalism live in our hearts, and they will fester whether or not we sleep under an open sky.

Instead, I want to offer the wisdom of Dionysus's probing, interrogative vine. What if we looked to plants for advice on how to revolt? What if we asked the Animate Everything for slippery suggestions? I am always drawn back to that life-affirming quote from activist Toni Cade Bambara: "The role of the artist is to make the revolution irresistible."[7] Responding to this approach, feminist writer adrienne maree brown invites us into "pleasure activism." How can our pleasure, our vine-like questioning and probing of the system, begin to confuse the systems that constrict us? How can we, like ivy, begin to encircle the hand that holds the sword, until it is so tightly bound it can't help but drop its weapon?

I'm not sure what the answer is, but I think by studying the invasive species in our local ecologies we can learn about subversive revolutionary tactics. What does it mean to digest a building? What if revolution involved sinking our hands into fresh loam and feeling for the threads of mycorrhizal fungi connecting plants and trees? What if, before we began to fight, we rooted back into our earth-based pleasure? We learn how to revolt when we make medicines from invasives and when we look curiously at what the land is doing, rather than immediately trying to "cure" it or clean it up. What does it mean to transform a polluted landscape into a healthy forest? The landscape knows better than us and will show us if we look closely enough.

I call on the vine and the ivy of Dionysus/Liber. And then I also summon the appetitive hyphae of Orpheus's mycelial underworld and the invasive mustard seeds of Jesus's kingdom. Let me call, too, on the muscular roots of the willow trees that sprang from the graves of the Dark Age heroes. Roots infamous for bursting through stone foundations. And I summon the wildflower pollen of ancient wounded gods.

Let it drift across our lawns and transform them into opalescent fields of purple and blue blooms. Make me a vine. A mushroom. An ashen root. A seed. Mold me into a resilience that is more tangled than a human myth, smaller than an atom, more melodious than a single word, or voice, or song.

14

Rewilding the Beloved

Dionysus Offers New Modes of Romance

Isn't it strange that the god of phallic wands, probing vegetation, wine, and lovemaking is often characterized in Western academic settings as asexual?

The argument is strange. Extraordinarily, Dionysus is one of the only—if not *the* only—Greek or Roman god who does not commit rape. There are no stories of him kidnapping women or assaulting women. Neither does he harm younger boys or men. This is one of the main arguments Western scholars use to argue that Dionysus is abstracted from actual sexuality and couldn't possibly be a virile, desirous lover. Unlike his father, Zeus, he doesn't trick or dupe or destroy women. He does not behave like the dominant patriarchal pantheon he is nestled inside. This simplification of Dionysus seems suspect to me. His femininity and androgyny, his long hair and strange dress, and the other measures of his "otherness" are also included in these attempts to neuter and erase a pre-patriarchal mode of the sexual masculine.

Why is masculinity conflated with dominance and violence? Why does the fact that Dionysus has no interest in domination mean he can't be a sexual, passionate lover? Why does his atypical physical presentation preclude him from sensuality? "Well, stranger, I see this body of yours is not unsuitable for women's pleasure," says the Theban king Pentheus in Ian Johnston's translation of *Bacchae*. "As for your hair, it's long, which suggests that you're no wrestler. It flows across your cheeks. That's most seductive. You've a white skin, too. You've looked after it."[1] What is it about Dionysus's unclassifiable beauty, his ability to inspire the appreciation of both women and men, that disturbs academics and kings alike?

Let me offer an alternative narrative. What if the fact that Dionysus does not need to commit rape or violent assault in order to attract lovers makes him even more masculine? What if the ease of his masculinity, the biodiversity of forms and possibilities he represents, causes the rigid and monolithic masculinity of patriarchy to contract around its lack of options? What if Dionysus is a window into a healthier, more fertile world of masculinities that existed before the Greek invasions of the Mediterranean Basin and the end of the Bronze Age? What if he was so sexually potent and self-assured that he didn't have to resort to patriarchal modes of repression and abuse? Dionysus is referred to as the god of women. Women were easily attracted to him and his flavor of ecstatic, nature-based spirituality. He didn't need to punish or force lovers into sexual submission. The lovers, women and men and satyrs and goddesses, were already fully ready to offer their affections.

The myths tell us Dionysus needed only to walk by a city in order to precipitate a wave of collective madness. A throng of desirous and adoring women, we are told by miffed male historians, would drop their chores and dignified dress and charge into the woods.

I'm reminded of the movie *Hard Day's Night,* about the Beatles: smooth-faced boys singing about love and attracting the frenzied adoration of hordes of girls. What lesson about love and romance does Dionysus deliver to us from his pre-patriarchal mycelium? What paleolithic lustiness can we drink from his deep kantharos?

Let's return to the Greek interpretation of the Minotaur, Ariadne, and Theseus. The cocky half-god Theseus comes to the island of Crete. He asserts that he can kill the monstrous brother of Ariadne who lives at the center of the labyrinth and devours human tributes. Here, let us remember that the Minotaur symbolizes all the earlier horned gods and bull gods of lunar partnership societies, where women and men alike honored nature as divine over and above anything else. Theseus has come to dominate and "rewrite" older narratives.

Ariadne, enchanted by the handsome Theseus, gifts him a ball of yarn that will safely lead him back out of the labyrinth after he has killed her brother. The yarn, here, is deeply symbolic. Weaving has always been associated with fate, storytelling, women's prophetic power, and the umbilical thread that ties a child to the womb.[2] When Ariadne gives Theseus her "yarn," she is giving him her story, her body, her connection to the mysteries of birth, and her red pulsing vein of power. Legends suggest that Theseus, after slaying the bull god, claims Ariadne sexually and romantically, leaving Crete with her. But, almost immediately, Theseus then abandons the lady of the labyrinth, leaving her sleeping on the shores of the island of Naxos.

I think most women, and plenty of other people, can imagine what this feels like. You wake up alone and perhaps scared. Maybe you're covered in fluid. Sea salt. Sand. Blood. Your own blood. And your lover whom you'd trusted—or your abuser—or both—is gone. Free from culpability. Free from answering for his violence against you.

In his first-century compendium of myths, Pseudo-Apollodorus tells us that as Ariadne tends to her heartbreak on the beach, bemoaning her foolishness in trusting the young patriarchal hero Theseus, Dionysus comes ashore, lured by the princess's beauty and strength. "Why are you crying?" he asks her. "Why would you mourn a man, when you could have a god, and be a goddess?"[3]

Not only does Dionysus woo and heal Ariadne and make her his beloved wife, he brings her up into the heavens and transforms her into a goddess with her own constellation. Ariadne, presumably the "lady of the labyrinth" of the ancient Minoan Linear B tablets, is given back her status as a goddess by Dionysus. If Theseus is a thief, having "stolen" her lunar bull gods, her access to her sacred labyrinth dance, then Dionysus is the great restorer. He heals her heart, and he recognizes, behind the smear campaign of dominant Greek narratives, her status as a sacred goddess of the earth.

My favorite aspect of their relationship is that in many stories and images—a wonderful example being the frieze from the Villa of the Mysteries in Pompeii—Ariadne is depicted as occupying the sovereign throne while Dionysus sits in her lap. Their relationship is flipped, dynamic, unfettered by gendered stereotypes. There is no dominating "king." Informed by an adaptogenic ability to bring balance to a disturbed ecosystem, Dionysus immediately corrects the power dynamic by elevating his beloved to divine status and giving her back her earthly throne and cosmic constellated crown.

At a time when one in three women have experienced sexual violence, Dionysus might be an important role model for the masculine. What does it mean to approach the beloved knowing that they have been wronged? What does it look like to tenderly heal that wounding and that power imbalance? My guess is the answer is more luscious and beautiful and sexy than we can even imagine. Healing doesn't have to be hard work. It can be romantic. It can be a bacchanal.

15

Grow Back Your Horns

The Devil Card Is Dionysus

You close your eyes, seeing black: the black of a black bear against the night, apparent only briefly, when moonlight strikes flintlike against the oiled fur along the bear's spine. You hear the darkness of sound: the loon's song tunneling through lake water, the velveteen thump of a humming-bird moth against the window. Petrichor: rain waking up the warm, deep scent of the soil. A lover's fingers pinching out the candle. The heft of overripe plums. Honey almost peppery with wildflower pollen. Walking inside the barn at night, animals shuffling against each other, cooing and mooing like blind electrons, dream-dancing around an atom.

Welcome to the Devil card.

Or, as he should be known, the Dionysus card.

For here is our favorite god of revolution, lovemaking, vegetation, soil, dance, and fermentation, thinly cloaked with Christian prejudice. Elaine Pagels maps the history of the Christian Devil in her book *The Origin of Satan*, demonstrating that pre-Christian Jewish ideas of devils were neutral or even positive.[1] And very often Devil imagery leads directly back to the worship of theriomorphic vegetal gods.

Originally, as Pagels tells us, the idea of "devil" had no theological baggage; it meant simply "stumbling block." The genderless figure of a devil was seen as a course correction. Something that blocks the wrong way forward. You are forced to stop and reassess. You step closer to your true desires and purpose as a result. This devil, then, is closer to the modern idea of the guardian angel. It shepherds you away from danger, sometimes loudly, sometimes gently. Pagels shows that as Christianity developed, it found a "scapegoat" in the goat-horned god Dionysus. Racism, misogyny, and anti-Semitism were poured into the now-singular Devil, who didn't represent evil so much as the bowl where the dominant culture could ferment its most violent prejudices.

We see traces of this history in the card itself. The horns, bat wings, and bird feet recall older pagan practices that venerated nature and animal gods. In the earliest depictions of the card, the Devil is most like the blended Dionysus: half animal, with both breasts and a phallus. The darkness of the Devil card is not the black of absence but the inky, living dirt with germinating seeds, sucking up moisture and nutrients to feed an entire forest. Simplistic interpretations of the Devil card warn of excess, overinflated egotism, and abuse of power. But the Devil as Dionysus is actually the antidote to these vices. These interpretations are misdirections from the true symbols of patriarchal capitalism: the Emperor, the Chariot, and the Hierophant. Let us entertain a new interpretation of this card. The Devil has been a dumping ground for hate and prejudice. But it has also been the place where older, more fertile practices have survived as stowaways.

Look at the Devil card and you will see the doubling of the Lovers card. Chained to a black block with the Devil crouching above them, two lovers incline their horned heads toward each other. They look at their shared chains. Some interpretations warn that the lovers have given into their animal instinct and fallen into "hedonism." If so, good for them. We could all use more animal instinct. We need to put our horns back on and start thinking less as individuals and more as patchy, contaminated relationships to other peoples, ecologies, and modes of consciousness.

In the Lovers card the man looks at the woman, while the woman stares away from him, up at a disembodied angel—a monotheistic sky deity. The lovers are not truly connected. They lack reciprocity.

Abstraction dominates. The woman looks at the sky and not at her feet or at her earthly partner. The lovers of the Devil card, by contrast, heal the Cartesian abstraction of the Lovers card. Both gaze at the chain that connects them. They incline their heads downward toward the earth and inward toward each other.

We are not mindless symbols, the card seems to say—not flat cards flying out of a deck. We are sticky, unruly relationships, intimately tied to the earth, to each other, and to those theriomorphic Dionysian deities that slip in and out of the imaginal realm when we need a "stumbling block" course correction. What if we reinterpreted the chains of the Devil card as mycelial rootlets? This is mushroom intelligence, linking and dispersing information. Probing and splitting. Slipping backward on itself. Involuting.

The lovers of the Devil card are rooted to the earth and to each other. They remind us that we haven't always been outside the garden. The garden is just below our feet. We don't need a grand spiritual awakening in order to come back into this Edenic consciousness. We just need to pay close, special attention to the connections that already constitute us. The lush, environmental contexts that shape our desires, our appetites, and our stories. Let us give thanks to the Devil card for holding hatred without dissolving underneath it. Let us thank this Dionysian goat-god for protecting the lovers below his bat wings, for helping them grow horns again, and teaching them how to send down roots.

I don't just want to reclaim the Devil for the masculine. I want to place him firmly between people, between plants, between lovers. He teaches us to grow connective tissue in soil through Indigenous land practices, soil regeneration, and the cultivation of native mycorrhizal communities. But he also, simply, heals our ability to love, not with our meatless language or our minds, but with our whole, messy, indeterminate, gender-flickering, bat-winged bodies.

PART II

HEALING THE WOUND

16

Let Your Wings Dry

Giving the Star Card to the Masculine

The night sky is elephant-skin blue, stippled with stars. The ground underfoot plush with moss and peat. Wild thyme, crushed, releases a bright yellow smell. You nearly mistake the giant sycamore for a muscular white snake, twisting toward the moon. But as you stop and place a hand to its flaking bark, you spot something in the branches. An ibis? A butterfly, blue with black-fringed wings?

Welcome to the Star card.

In variations of the tarot going back to Bonifacio Bembo's original illustrations, we see a figure (man or woman, depending on the deck) with two vessels, pouring water into a pool with one hand and water onto fertile, welcoming earth with the other.[1] One foot rests in the shallows, and the other slips into the dirt and wild grasses of the landscape. Typically, the figure is naked, circled by seven stars, a fact that calls to mind the seven chakras for some tarot readers. An ibis or a butterfly rests in the foliage of a distant tree. The scene is tranquil but dynamic. Energy moves within a closed circuit. Water flows into water.

Classically, the card is related to healing. The woman pictured pours "cleansing waters" over wounds. But in a culture where healing is disregarded in favor of speed and progress, that healing becomes much harder to accept. Women receive scant maternity leave. Unable to pay for health care, people slap bandages on mortal wounds, desperately fearing emergency-room bills. Others ignore the fire alarms screaming in their own bodies and show up to work, day after day, until they keel over and die. This isn't to mention the spiritual and psychological wounding from centuries of patriarchal domination, colonization, genocide, and ecocide. Even our religions and mythologies have been steadily hemorrhaging, unable to pause and let the cut close and scab over. We leave Christ up on the cross. We let Attis and Adonis bleed into wildflower patches. We ignore centuries of systematic genocide. Anti-Semitic massacres. Indigenous people wiped out. Whole villages of women, nonbinary people, and "heretics" tortured and burned and massacred. No wonder we suffer from anxiety attacks and a nagging sense of existential dread.

Deep, ragged wounds cannot be immediately stitched closed. If they are closed without healing from inside outward, they can putrefy and cause sepsis. Instead, they must be kept clean and open, with muscle and tissue reknitting from the bottom up until finally smoothing into a scar. This is not a quick fix. It is a long, careful process. Healing cannot be rushed. It is not a superficial process. It has to happen from the roots.

When we pull the Star card, it offers the patience needed to let a wound heal from the bottom up. The body and the psyche's pace is distinctly opposed to the culture's suicidal sprinting. I think the Star card is a card of healing, but it is the deep healing that cannot be rushed. I think of the powerful advice from John O'Donohue in his poem "For the Interim Time":

> *What is being transfigured here is your mind,*
> *And it is difficult and slow to become new.*
> *The more faithfully you can endure here,*
> *The more refined your heart will become*
> *For your arrival in the new dawn.*[2]

At its core, healing is transformation. Broken skin grows new cells. Bones melt into new shapes. A scar creates a striking rosy tattoo, a silkier texture. A body that has been through illness understands its shape, its limitations, its pleasure, with an almost excruciating precision. Likewise, emotional and psychological healing helps us shed old patterns and coping mechanisms, emerging into a vital, new self. But as O'Donohue writes, "It is difficult and slow to become new."

Here, let us think of the dragonfly's metamorphosis. This is not like the simple caterpillar to cocoon to butterfly. No. The dragonfly's transformation is agonizingly slow. A prolarva bursts from its egg, searches for water, then hatches and molts. But this is just the beginning of the journey. The larva will hatch and molt another five to fourteen times, sometimes spending up to five years in the process of becoming. Finally, after having shed not one version of itself, but many, the larva crawls into shallower water, poking its head up and slowly tasting air. It breathes for the first time under cover of darkness. When it has literally caught its breath, it drags its wet body onto land, climbing up a flower stalk or hardy blade of grass where it can rest. When it has secured itself, it totally redistributes the liquid of its body, beginning to push out of itself. Once out of the "exuvia" of shed skin, the slimy, shiny dragonfly waits for its legs to harden and its wings to dry. The emergence process takes up to three hours, usually timed for the early morning.[3]

The Star card welcomes us into the murky waters of slow, transformative healing. As men try to attend to the wounds of patriarchy, the wounds they have inflicted on others and on themselves, the roles they are trying to shed, the roles they are trying to expand into, it is important to remember that real healing cannot be rushed. If we don't emerge slowly from the shallows, we won't give our lungs time to adjust to the intoxicating chill of fresh air. If we don't give our wings time to dry, we will never be able to fly. Stepping out of dominant cultural narratives involves a process of grieving, tending to our losses, and transforming our dreams. This doesn't happen in an hour. And it can't be "gamed."

Instead, it involves a compassionate, daily check-in. How am I feeling? Do I need to move more slowly?

The Star card invites men to the shore. Put one foot in the water and keep the other firmly planted in the dirt. Feel your bothness. The movement and slipperiness of the water. The steady, resilient, mycelial intelligence of the soil between your toes. The dominant culture would have us believe that healing must be bought. That it can only be prescribed by people with degrees. Modern medicine, including psychiatry, cannot be discounted in its achievements, but it is important to remember that the natural world has always been our chrysalis. It has always been our transformative medicine. As men move into new modes of the masculine and sense that it is time to shed an old skin, to heal a wound from the bottom up, they need only step outside and request tenderly: "Please hold me during this time. Please move me slowly and lovingly into newness."

17

Tristan and Transformation

Escaping the Trauma of the Hero's Journey

Who lives in sorrow is like a man dead. And he desired some death . . .

JOSEPH BÉDIER,
THE ROMANCE OF TRISTAN AND ISEULT

Tristan is dying to escape. Literally dying or trying to. He throws himself off cliffs, out of church windows, off boats, into impossible battles, and, most often, out into the dark night of a stormy ocean.

Tristan, a Dark Age romantic hero, is known for his doomed love for the Irish princess Isolde, who is married to his friend King Mark. The story plays on themes of duty and love, and the central love triangle may have formed the basis of the later Arthurian myths.

From his birth onward, Tristan is constantly running away from typical manhood. When his parents King Rivalin and Queen Blancheflor die, Tristan is adopted by a lower-rank friend of his father who hides Tristan's real identity. As a boy he runs off (or is kidnapped by pirates after a betrayal by his stepbrothers) and washes up on the shores of Cornwall, escaping his adoptive father's stultifying belief that Tristan must be educated and made into a "noble" knight. Tristan rises to fame in the court of King Mark (the sixth-century king of Cornwall) through a distinctly paleolithic power: his knowledge of the hunt and the ways of the deer. But the minute his royal ancestry is acknowledged and it seems he might have to become the king of Lyonesse, or worse, Mark's heir, Tristan knows he must escape.

A musician and a trickster, Tristan does not want to ascend to patriarchal power. Instead, he gives his father's kingdom to his adoptive father and escapes Mark's attempt to make him an heir by throwing himself into a suicidal battle with the Irish warrior Morholt. Victorious, but fatally wounded by a poisoned sword wound in the groin, Tristan is faced with two fates: to die inside the sterile masculine archetype or to surrender to the ocean of something older and wilder. Tristan, ever the anti-hero, asks his friends to secretly send him out to sea in the middle of the night with no oars and only his harp. He leaves behind the phallic sword and puts his trust in melody, in rhythm rather than rigidity. He trusts the ocean. Most of all, he trusts his own poisoned wound. And like the Greek word *pharmakon,* which indicated a substance both poison and medicine, Tristan's poison is also the medicine that will cure the traumatic wounding of a hero's solitary journey toward domination and death.[1]

Morholt's sword carried a poison that leads Tristan back to the land of his original legend: Ireland. Ireland, where paganism had been semiprotected from the Romans and Christianity. Where the Goddess still knew how to transform narcissistic heroes into fertile magicians. Waiting for Tristan on the Irish shore are two women. One older, one younger, mother and daughter, they echo the older Bronze Age double goddess: Demeter and Persephone, who manifest now as Queen Isolde and her daughter Princess Isolde. The women pull him out of the ocean and wash him free of his name. When he recovers Tristan calls himself by a new name, Tantris, and offers his service as a music teacher to the lovely princess.

So begins Tristan's healing. He will no longer be shackled to violence and domination. By leaving behind his sword, he is transformed into an older kind of masculine archetype, one that tells a story with cunning and magic and music. What seems deeply important is that, in most of the textual versions of the legend, after this wounding and night sea journey, Tristan is no longer primarily referred to as a knight or associated with battle. No. He is most often referred to as a sorcerer, magician, or harpist. An Orpheus. A lover.

Yet sorrow is Tristan's burden and birthright. He not only lives in sorrow, he is called it, since his name derives from the French word *triste,* "sorrow." He was given his name after his mother, Blancheflor, died in childbirth following the news that her beloved husband, Rivalin, had died in battle.

How long does it take someone to outrun their name? The answer to this question, for Tristan, is famously tragic. While he evades death multiple times—poisoned by Morholt's spear, jumping from clifftops, and escaping King Mark's wrath when he learns his wife Isolde has betrayed him with Tristan—he cannot escape forever. Finally, wounded in a petty skirmish with neighboring tribes, Tristan dies heartbroken, fevered, and disgraced, with his beloved only miles away.

Isolde, his great love, is still married to King Mark, but hearing that Tristan is near death, she quickly hops on a boat. She is a great healer and knows she may be able to save her lover. But she is too late. Many suppose that if Isolde had made it to Tristan's bedside in time, the talented Irish herbalist would have been able to save her beloved. But perhaps we should admit that Tristan was already doomed. There are only so many wounds—psychic and physical—someone can hold before deciding that they can't keep walking, that they can't keep letting the narrative roll them onward.

Mythically, we think of Tristan as a handsome knight of love, a proto-troubadour with shiny armor and luscious locks. Gottfried von Strassburg describes him as "smooth and soft," with hands as "white as ermine."[2] King Mark's fascination with Tristan's wit and beauty always borders on erotic, as does the enchantment of Tristan's tutor, Governal, and his friend Caerdin. His allure is playful androgyny. He is both pretty and quick. Boyish, but mature in battle and bed. He plays the harp and often disguises himself as a fool. He invites role reversals from his lovers, the most memorable episode being when Isolde surprises Tristan taking a bath and threatens him with a knife to his throat.

But let us halt the story, because stories are often defense mechanisms used to distract from pain. Trauma can look like heroism. It can look like strength. Sound like beautiful music. It can be handsome and well behaved. What beautiful Tristan really represents is pain.

Tristan, born of heartbreak, dives immediately into a series of traumatic events. He is betrayed by his stepbrothers, kidnapped by pirates, and then seriously wounded by Morholt. Interestingly, Tristan seems almost relieved when he receives the "stinking" wound. His trauma, so long invisible, is finally clear to all. Everyone can see it. In fact, everyone can smell it. The wound literally emits a foul scent. He can finally rest, surrender, and put himself out to sea.

So often our wounding goes unseen and unacknowledged to the point that it becomes somatized—that is, expressed through somatic symptoms. As research into post-traumatic stress disorder has shown, a dysregulated nervous and immune system can begin to manifest real wounds to match emotional pain. Survivors of trauma and abuse are much more likely to develop terminal autoimmune and neurological disorders. It is telling that as Tristan's psychic wounds accumulate, so do his physical wounds. Somatic experts Bessel van der Kolk and Peter Levine warn against the "desperate compulsion for reenactment."[3] Tristan re-creates wounds to signal that he cannot continue at breakneck speed through narrative episode after episode.

Tristan's wound is personal as well as mythic. Wounded in the groin, he calls to mind Attis and Adonis, killed by boars during the hunt. He prefigures the Fisher King and Wolfram von Eschenbach's

Amfortas, languishing in the Grail castle. But perhaps most fittingly, he reminds us of the wounded Chiron, half man and half horse. Throughout the story, Tristan tries to return to his "wilder" half by seeking out the forest or the sea. Just as Tristan's body is wounded, so is his narrative. He is a Celtic pagan hero, deeply tied to the environment, wrenched from his homeland and reinserted into a civilized Christian romance more interested in "duty" than in sacred ecology. Little surprise, then, that our hero is hobbled. His wounds are stratigraphic. Layer upon layer.

As he is thrown into one event after the other, Tristan is never allowed the slow, nonlinear, nonnarrative time it takes to heal. Words aren't always the best way to access pain. Sometimes the story doesn't staunch the bleeding heart. In his seminal work on somatics, *Waking the Tiger,* Peter Levine writes, "I learned that it was unnecessary to dredge up old memories and relive their emotional pain to heal trauma. In fact, severe emotional pain can be re-traumatizing. What we need to do to be freed from our symptoms is . . . to arouse our deep physiological resources and consciously utilize them."[3]

So much of the current rhetoric about healing is wedded to progress and to narrative. But the body is not a story. It is porous and complicated and changeable. It needs to dance and swim. It needs to lie on the ground for days, re-regulating its nervous system to the seasonal heartbeat of the soil. The concept of "healing" has become the time-sensitive demand of a culture bent on progressing, and unwittingly taken up by wellness and new age spiritual communities. They say we must be "integrated" and whole again; we must achieve functionality so that we can keep the narrative moving. But a body doesn't need to move through healing. It just needs to move. And then it needs to be still. It needs to feel safe.

As we look back on centuries of violence and oppression and begin to confront the very real wounds we have inflicted on the land and on each other, it is important that we don't try to accelerate through the difficulty. We must, as Donna Haraway so elegantly puts it, "stay with the trouble."[4] Ultimately, sorrow is not healed. It is held. It is honored. It is melted and blended. It moves with the body, not through linear episodes, but through slow, conscious, spiraled dance. As men acknowledge the harm they have done to others and to each other, it is important that they check in with their bodies and the greater body of the earth. Let us take Tristan and put him on a hill with a cup of tea. Let us tell him he can be still for as long as he likes. For right now, he doesn't need to save anybody. He doesn't even need to save himself.

18

Boy David, Wild David, King David

The Land-Based Origin of Biblical Kingship

And it came to pass, when the evil spirit from God was upon Saul, that David took an harp, and played with his hand: so Saul was refreshed, and was well, and the evil spirit departed from him.

1 SAMUEL 16:23

"I cannot walk in these. I am not accustomed to them," David insists when King Saul tries to outfit him in his personal armor (1 Samuel 17:39).

The young boy takes off the armor and approaches the Philistine giant Goliath "naked," except for a handful of smooth stones, a stick, and his shepherd's slingshot. In order to come into his power, and his divinely ordained kingship, David must embrace profound vulnerability. He must approach the impossible without any hardness, without any patriarchal adornment. What if becoming king means taking off all the "accessories" of kingship? What if it means showing up completely naked?

Reading King David as an antipatriarchal figure seems counter-intuitive. The second king of Israel is best known for his skill as a brutal warrior and for his extramarital affairs. But it is important to note that the Book of Samuel and the entire Deuteronomistic history of the Hebrew Bible were composed around 630 to 540 BCE from oral traditions and competing textual accounts, and further edited during the Jewish Babylonian exile.[1] The story of David has been uprooted, translated to suit anachronous political motivations, and molded to fit a patriarchal narrative.

Luckily, it appears that David has not been entirely compliant with his monotheistic makeover. There are crucial hints in his story that we are looking at a Neolithic hero rather than an Iron Age king. This is a boy of the fields, rather than a sovereign of the city-state.

The story begins with the prophet Samuel's divine revelation that King Saul is unfit for ruling Israel. Instead, God instructs him to look to the sons of a man called Jesse for the new king. Unfortunately, Jesse has eight sons, and Samuel, prophet of the budding patriarchy, is problematically keyed toward a narrow idea of masculinity. Saul himself is a handsome and tall man: "There was not among the children of Israel a goodlier [more handsome] person than he: from his shoulders and upward he was higher than any of the people" (1 Samuel 9:2).

Looking for another classical king, Samuel immediately picks out Jesse's oldest and tallest son, Eliab. Thankfully, God intervenes with an older, Neolithic sensibility. He instructs Samuel: "Look not on his countenance, or on the height of his stature; because I have refused him: for the Lord seeth not as man seeth" (1 Samuel 16:7). Instead, he advises, Samuel should see from "the heart."

Luckily, one son is absent from the kingship audition: the youngest son, David. As is the case in many fairy tales, refusing the call is a prerequisite for the sovereign role. David doesn't believe there is any chance that he will be the king, establishing a theme of humility that will thread through his entire narrative. In Psalm 22:6, attributed to the poet-king, he writes, "But I am a worm, and no man." A simplistic modern morality has us read this as modesty. But I think there is a deeper undercurrent to David's reluctance to overidentify with the spoils of patriarchal kingship.

Myths are so often abstracted from their original ecosystems, languages, and peoples that it is important, when possible, to recontextualize them.

What information is initially attached to the figure of David? A field. He is outside—outside the roll call for kingship and outside the political system. Instead, he is housed in landscape, surrounded by his sheep. His initial "attributes" are the outdoors and animals. So, when we hear David call himself a worm later on in the Psalms, underneath the self-negation, I pick up on an intimacy with the earth and an acknowledgment that his narrative birthplace is the fields, external to the world of men.

Not only is David literally outside in the fields, but he—the very king who became emblematic of dynastic Jewish lineage—was himself of uncertain lineage. David was the great-grandson of a converted Moabite woman, Ruth, a fact that was hotly debated as he rose to power. Rather arbitrarily, it was finally agreed by rabbinical consensus that a convert grandmother was acceptable, but if it had been his great-grandfather, he would have been disqualified as ruler of the Jewish people. Not only is his background hazy, but David does not look like a classical tall, dark Jewish king. He is noted as being very good-looking, but "ruddy" and with "fair eyes." By comparison with his taller brothers, we can infer that he was of small stature. This all amounts to the picture of a pretty, slight, blue-eyed redhead emerging from the fields covered in grass and smelling like the sheep he sleeps beside.

David, then, appears to be a rhizomatic fruiting of the underground system of lunar kings, magical musicians, and horned gods of the Neolithic and the Bronze Age. He comes from the forest. The wild. He will be king of men, but his right to kingship erupts from the landscape itself.

⁓

It is important to note that the Judaism that was practiced contemporaneously with David's rise to power was not the strict monotheism we identify as Judaism today.[2] It was still an assemblage of oral, folkloric traditions directly related to early pantheistic Canaanite religions. Robert Alter, professor of Hebrew studies expands on archaeological evidence to show that many northwest Semitic gods developed from sacred mountains.[3] David comes from a Judaism that is still deeply animistic and pluralistic. The monotheistic themes of the Book of Samuel are more indicative of the religion of its authors than the historical time period they were narrativizing.

Nowhere is this more apparent than in David's famous confrontation with Goliath (1 Samuel 17). Too young and scrawny to fight the Philistines, he is sent by his father with "ten wedges of cheese" for his older brothers at the front line. The largest and fiercest of the Philistines, a giant named Goliath, has challenged the Israelites to decide the conflict in single combat. When David hears about the challenge from Goliath, he immediately offers himself up for the task: "What shall be done to the man that killeth this Philistine, and taketh away the reproach from Israel? . . . Let no man's heart fail because of him; thy servant will go and fight with this Philistine." Naturally, everyone doubts the young boy's ability. King Saul scoffs, "Thou art but a youth, and he a man of war from his youth."

Not only is David young, but he is a lowly shepherd, untrained as a warrior.

David is unfazed, explaining that, while he may not have received training in battle, he has been well taught by wilder teachers. David is no gentleman warrior. He has learned war from the beasts. As a shepherd, he regularly had to fend off dangerous animals to protect his flock: "Thy servant kept his father's sheep, and there came a lion, and a bear, and took a lamb out of the flock: And I went out after him, and smote him, and delivered it out of his mouth: and when he arose against me,

I caught him by his beard, and smote him, and slew him. Thy servant slew both the lion and the bear." David comes from a bestial lineage. He is feral, associated with animal strength and intelligence. His preparation for both battle and kingship has, like the boy Arthur transmogrified by the wizard Merlin in T. H. White's *The Once and Future King,* come from the world of the fields, the lions, and the bears.

Even as David acclimates to sovereignty and the concerns of men, he maintains a direct link to the animistic currents of the landscape. During battle his messages from God come in the form of "the sound of a going in the tops of the mulberry trees" (2 Samuel 5:24). David is a lion wrestler and a tree reader. The strange phrase "sound of a going" refers to the movement of wind through leaves. The divine is movement, the blended essence of tree and breath itself.

It is fitting, then, that after David has defeated Goliath with skill and a stone, the text tells us, "There was no sword in the hand of David." David, while he will use a sword and, apparently, kill thousands more than his predecessor Saul, does not begin his story with a sword. Although he enters into patriarchy, he does not begin in patriarchy. This is an important lesson for the masculine. Yes, we are *in* patriarchy. But that is not where we began.

We began in the fields. With the sheep. And the lions. And the bears. Before he was a warrior and a king, David was something else. He was a musician.

David's initiation into the royal sphere is by way of his lyre playing and poetic intelligence. King Saul is informed that David is "skilled in playing and . . . prudent in speech" (1 Samuel 16:18). While Saul and David's relationship will eventually sour, it begins intimately in the vibrations of one of the oldest mythic instruments: the lyre.[4] God, annoyed that Saul has not followed all his instructions, tells the prophet Samuel that Saul no longer has his endorsement. Saul, depressed by his divine rejection, can only be soothed by the playing of the youthful musician.

In *The David Story,* Robert Alter notes that David's narrative debut as slayer of Goliath mirrors a classical fairy-tale structure. An anonymous boy, unassuming in appearance, defeats a dragon or monsters threatening a kingdom. But what if the flashy nature of the giant slaying has obscured the most potent aspect of David's story?

An anonymous boy with a divinely sponsored claim to kingship enchants a king with his lyre playing. They form an intimate bond. The boy then challenges a giant to a battle. Impossibly, the boy is victorious. Later, the king, jealous of the popularity of the boy warrior, will seek to kill him. The boy will flee into exile in order to save himself.

If the story sounds familiar, that is because it doesn't belong just to King David. It is also the exact narrative framework of the Tristan and Isolde myth.

Tristan enters anonymously into the court of King Mark, gaining the intimate friendship of the king by enchanting him with his "excellent sweet music" that made any man listening "forget his name." Like David, Tristan's instrument of seduction is the lyre. Slender, smooth-handed, and unassuming like the young David, Tristan does not present as a talented warrior. But this doesn't dissuade him from challenging his own Goliath, the fearsome Irish warrior Morhault, to a battle that no one believes he can win. Victorious, Tristan gains the respect of King Mark's subjects, a fact that makes the king uneasy. And later Tristan, too, will be forced into exile to escape the wrath of the king he once counted as his friend.

The lyric, nature-oriented trickster quality of the boy represents older egalitarian societies as opposed to the jealous, dominating rule of the king. The character dynamics easily map onto the historical tension between pantheistic goddess cultures and the rise of monotheistic patriarchies.

Tristan will become the prototype for the Romances of the troubadours. Many scholars have rigorously shown that the Arthurian legends are translations of earlier versions of the Tristan myths. But I want to argue that Tristan is a translation of someone much earlier still. What if the Romances emerged from deep underground?

What if their initial mythic mycelium wasn't in Europe but deep in the Mediterranean?

It seems obvious that Tristan is David. Even Joseph Campbell noted that the similarity between the two heroes was striking. David, mythologically if not historically, will "author" the biblical Psalms, making him an early hero of lyric poetry.[5] Tristan is the inheritor of David's narrative. But he also inherits a great gift—the gift of an older, pre-patriarchal mode of masculinity.

Both young men show that real power is derived from music and poetry. The way to enter into a new story is by way of the lyre. You don't have to slay the kings of patriarchy. You just have to charm and seduce them into listening to you. And then, when you have everyone's attention, you start to sing a different sort of story. A romance. A ballad of boys who wrestle bears. A music that still remembers how to hear a god speaking through the trees.

19

Coppice the Hero's Journey

Creating Narrative Ecosystems

It is ironic that Joseph Campbell's favorite hero, Tristan, is so desperate to escape the very thing Campbell wanted to enshrine him inside: the hero's journey.[1]

For Campbell, the Tristan myth signaled a move away from an earlier collective mysticism into a new view of creative individualistic mythology and romance. Individuals made their own myths. Men were heroes, heading out into the forest, where it was darkest and thickest, to author and conquer their own valorous, rugged story. The forest became the other, the oppositional force that tempers the hero into an alchemical kingship. The forest, the natural realm, becomes a thing to be entered, struggled against, and dominated, rather than the very matrix and mother of mythology itself.

A man sets out on a quest. He encounters dragons. Distressed maidens. Riddling wizards. Through a combination of cunning and brute strength, he reaches individual glory. The framework is familiar because it has been the most popular narrative frame for masculinity since the Middle Ages. But is the hero's journey still a useful story?

At the beginning of *The Hero with a Thousand Faces,* his seminal book about the hero's journey, Campbell writes:

The hero, therefore, is the man or woman who has been able to battle past his personal and local historical limitations to the generally valid, normally human forms. Such a one's visions, ideas, and inspirations come pristine from the primary springs of human life and thought. Hence they are eloquent, not of the present, disintegrating society and psyche, but of the unquenched source through which society is born.

The writing is clean and convincing. Society and purity are prized over darkness and uncertainty. *Eloquence,* that loaded word used to silence those who speak differently than the educated elite, is the hero's gift, and a battle through linear time is his story.

Campbell's theory of the monomyth was convincing enough that, although it faced much criticism, the hero's journey has infiltrated the very pith of our literature, our entertainment, and our psychosocial narratives. Even sperm have been transformed into little questing knights, journeying through the dark forest of the cervix until they can fertilize the egg, epitomized by Campbell's idea of key episodes common to all hero narratives: "meeting the goddess" and "woman as temptress."

But the hero's journey isn't always the best fit. Contrary to popular belief, eggs are the dominant force when it comes to fertilization, actively choosing which sperm they will attract and allow to implant.[2] Now that we know better, what does the egg's story sound like? What does it feel like to stand still and replete in your power to choose, not running off into the forest to slay dragons?

What does it feel like, as someone who identifies as a man, to be given only one story?

Is the hero's journey big enough for the current moment? I think not. Not even the neo-Darwinian idea of linear evolution has proved infallible, increasingly melting into questions of horizontal gene transfer and symbiogenesis.[3] In a moment when the technologies of the Anthropocene project us millions of years into the future and core us through deep time into glacial pockets of fungal breath from prototaxites in the Late Devonian period, we have to admit that our world is not a linear romp, with cardboard cut-out temptresses, riddling dragons, and singular heroes, into civilized eloquence. It is a polytemporal explosion of contingencies and sorrows and contamination.

A species of wild lupine dies and suddenly the Karner blue butterfly cannot lay her eggs. Overharvesting of horseshoe crabs disrupts the crucial rest and feeding opportunity of the red knot bird's continent-long migration. What is the journey of synchronous relationships, delicately attuned to the seasons and other beings' appetites? How can multiple stories with competing needs live together simultaneously?

Anthropologist Anna Lowenhaupt Tsing offers a compelling approach. She stresses that we must investigate "assemblages" over decontextualized individuals: "Assemblages are open-ended gatherings. They allow us to ask about communal effects without assuming them. They show us potential histories in the making."⁴ She encourages us to think of assemblages as polyphonies: beings interact and create music that condenses into beauty, then just as quickly pass back into clamor through unintentional yet coordinated behaviors.

Ecosystems are assemblages. And we, bodies with more microbial cells than human cells, are also assemblages. A happening. A polyphony of different, sometimes intertwining, sometimes dissonant, songs. This is a narrative possibility that, unlike Campbell's purity and eloquence, embraces complexity: the disabled, the queer, the refugees, the inhuman, the viral, the very tangled and overlapping relationships that bring us into situated existence.

How can we write ecosystems rather than individuals? A hero's journey implies a singular hero and a linear path. How can we write stories with crisscrossing paths? How can we write stories that reflect the messy, intertangled reality of living inside an ecosystem alongside many other species?

The idea of the assemblage is just one narrative option—and substituting one monomyth for another is not the answer to the poverty of narrative imagination facing the mythic masculine. We need to offer the masculine many different modes of narrative expression.

A *holobiont* is an assemblage of beings that creates a larger whole. The word was first used in 1991 by Lynn Margulis in an attempt to explain her study of hosts and inherited symbionts.[5] With each passing day new research confirms that macroorganisms like us human beings are intimately tuned and shaped by the populations of microbes and fungi (or, as microbiologist Siv Watkins calls them, "smalls") that populate our bodies. Our very cells were created by the fusion of ancient free-living prokaryotes. The closer we look at our bodies, the flimsier the idea of an individual, bounded self becomes. We are walking communities, swarms in suits and ties, skin-silhouetted Towers of Babel.

Perhaps, then, it is time to expand our idea of archetypes. Jungian archetypes are defined as ancient, universal ideas, modes of thought, or symbols that flower from the collective unconscious. These archetypes inhabit our myths and folklore. And the belief is that, over the course of our lives, we tend to embody different archetypes. Unfortunately, as happens with most attempts at mythical taxonomy, the idea of the archetype has become a sort of prison. We are the mother, the maid, or the crone. The anima or the shadow. Always an individual, always firmly within a codified state. The masculine, in particular, has been impoverished by the rigidity of certain archetypal approaches. What is the masculine allowed? King, warrior, magician, lover. I am, of course, referring to the popular book by Jungian analysts Robert Moore and Douglas Gillette, *King, Warrior, Magician, Lover,* wherein the authors argue that to be an integrated man, you must "master" these archetypes.

Little surprise, then, that when confronted with such an impoverished selection, men are often easily shoved into the unspoken fifth and sixth options: the villain and the fool. But the masculine is not just four storybook characters. The masculine is numerous. And, most importantly, the masculine is not one star in the sky; it is a constellation of relationships, rather than a concrete singular. We are teeming cauldrons of aliveness. Holobionts. We need better ways of talking about archetypal expressions.

Let us offer the tarot as vital nourishment to the masculine. I don't want to throw out the king, the warrior, the magician, and the lover. I just want to add more archetypes to create a biodiversity of masculinities. A holobiont that can thrive, flexibly dance with change, and evolve. Like most mythologies, the tarot comes to us from beyond the horizon of "proof." Some claim it began in Egypt. Others say it is a distinctly Kabbalistic practice. We know that the earliest tarot deck, distinct from other "playing cards," was designed by a mysterious man called Bonifacio Bembo in Milan in the mid-fifteenth century.

What I find particularly juicy about the tarot is that it is not one myth, it is many, and the modes of interpretation vary from reader to reader. The cups suit is its own cosmogony. The swords another. The Major Arcana can be read like a story. Each of the seventy-eight cards is a door to its own world. The deck is often used as an oracle, but I find it more exciting as a projective tool. We can pull four cards and think, "What does this constellation of images bring into focus? What conversation are these four cards having with each other?" When I read for other people, I try to show them that they are not *one* card. Each person is the messy, interconnected animacy of several different cards. We don't need to integrate these dissonant beings into one homogenized self. Instead, we can delight in the freedom to be unclassifiable, queer, in movement, and in process all at once. The entanglement of a tarot reading feels more generative and more closely aligned to the complexity we are beginning to explore in our own bodies and minds.

I am reminded of my favorite sylvan metaphor: the coppiced tree. Coppicing is the ancient practice of cutting a tree down to its stump, or stool, as it's known. Young tree stems then erupt from the single stool. The method, which has been a mainstay of woodland management across Europe for hundreds of years, has been utilized by many different Indigenous peoples the world over, and it is a key practice in the "peasant" satoyama forests of Japan, in which one tree is harvested for a modest requirement of firewood or building material, and six shoots take its place.[6]

The sight of a coppiced tree has always twinkled in my poet's mind, reminding me that we are never limited to a binary, never stuck to one "tree" or one course of action. Sometimes we need to cut down the tree of a monomythic idea in order to get to the more generative roots belowground that will spring into a polyphony of trunks aboveground. I'm not saying we need to throw out the hero's journey. But we do need a biodiversity of stories. We need multiple sprouts from one trunk. We need stories that don't center around human beings. And we need stories that do center around human beings. This is an invitation to cut back our ideas of linear progress and battle. To soften into the yellow sap of our stump for a moment. And then to begin talking and singing and sprouting into as many stories as there are spores on the wind, bacteria in our gut, unsung loves in the forgotten corner of our feral hearts.

I am gifting all seventy-eight cards of the tarot to the masculine. That's seventy-eight new nourishing archetypes. And I invite you to let yourself live interstitially, in the relationships and dissonance that emerge between two cards. Honor your wild, many-hued, holobiont selves.

20
Merlin and Vortigern
Magical Boyhood Topples Patriarchy

Vortigern, the mythic fifth-century English warlord, has a lot of problems. He has been driven into northern Britain by the Saxons he unwittingly invited into his country. His own people, the Welsh, are also angry at him. His offense is incest. Or perhaps it is stealing a Saxon wife? The story is muddled. Still, the major themes are war, women as chattel, and civil unrest in the wake of Roman imperialism. The biggest problem, however, is that every time Vortigern tries to build his new tower, it crumbles overnight. His court sorcerers advise him to find a fatherless child. Only the spilled blood of such a boy will rectify the instability of the tower's foundations, they say.

Unfortunately for Vortigern, the fatherless child he summons to be his sacrificial lamb is none other than the fourteen-year-old Merlin.

The historicity of Vortigern is debatable. He is mentioned by all the proto-historians: Gildas, Bede, Nennius, Geoffrey of Monmouth. But Vortigern is most interesting not as an isolated figure, but in his relationship to the mythical boy Merlin. This Merlin is partially a creation of Geoffrey of Monmouth and partially the final destination of the folkloric figure Emrys/Ambrosius. The oral legends of Emrys/Ambrosius had been circulating for hundreds of years before Geoffrey, the historian with a fictional flourish, firmly anchored the episode in Merlin mythology.

And Merlin never obeys the logic of patriarchy. He always comes to us from the woods. In this episode he comes to us from an even more magical place: boyhood. When the king summons him, Merlin quickly turns his death sentence on its head, scoffing at the king. "Who instructed you to do this?" he asks Vortigern. "My wise men," the king responds. Merlin confidently snaps, "Order them hither."

The symbolism is easy enough to read. A "fatherless" child is a child outside of patriarchal monotheism. A child with an allegiance to the mother. When Merlin bests the wise men and instructs them to dig below the tower, revealing a dragon's nest, the child of matriarchy reveals the "snakes" below the foundations of this new paradigm. These dragons are easily connected to the snake goddesses Tiamat, Inanna, Cybele, the Lady of the Labyrinth, Eve, and Medusa.[1] Merlin simply reveals the chthonic earth beings of an older, healthier humanity. The dragons have been suppressed by the Romans, and then by the patriarchal warlords, but not very well, and this tension is what keeps toppling Vortigern's tower.

The tower is easily read as phallus or sky penetrator, a singular monument to monotheism. The tower crumbles because it is built on the very matter/mother it is trying so desperately to erase. Merlin acts as an emissary from an earlier age, showing the "underworld" of an earlier belief system that must still be honored and acknowledged. It is from this katabatic descent that he draws his magical inspiration. Once he has revealed the dragons, the boy's story blooms into a prophecy that defies classification. Snakes and animals dominate, occasionally overlapping with the drama of the human world. The text has proved a fertile ground for exegesis, constantly appropriated and updated by kings, scholars, and authors to explain their current climate.[2]

But the real wisdom of this episode lies in Merlin's youth. This is not the white-bearded madman but the bright-eyed boy.

Merlin's predicament seems inescapable. But his childish mind opens a different option—a trapdoor in the literal foundations of Vortigern's tower. This is a power available to all children; as Robert Macfarlane writes in his enchanting book *Landmarks,* "To young children, of course, nature is full of doors—is nothing but doors, really. . . . What we bloodlessly call 'place' is to young children a wild compound of dream, spell, and substance."[3] Referring to the work of educator Deb Wilenski, making creative maps with schoolchildren, Macfarlane observes: "None of the doors the children drew . . . had locks. The doors appeared and disappeared, but always opened both ways."

Opening both ways is a skill we need to cultivate. We need to acknowledge the dragons in the foundation and the land-based nourishment they still have to offer us even after centuries of repression. But we must also slip through the door into the present moment and into the ever ripening tomorrow. The door that opens both ways might be the union of elders and children in a mutual act of oral storytelling. Oral storytelling with children, especially boys, would seem to be one of the ways we can escape the death sentence of patriarchy. How can we approach young boys as formidable magicians with vital wisdom to share?

Merlin's story appears fixed. But then he shoots back with the transformative question: "Who told you this?" Who does this story belong to? Can we tell a different one? A written story becomes fixed, but a spoken question invites a response. The rhythm of call and response, collaborative creating, can show us that even when we feel stuck, there is always a trapdoor. A new story to tell.

Patriarchal capitalism is the tower that keeps falling down. The earth itself is the foundation, destabilized by man-made climate change. If we stay in the tower and inside our brittle narratives, we risk our lives. But there are trapdoors everywhere. They are our relationships: to our ecosystems, to animals and fungi and plants, and to children. Children haven't yet learned that miracles and magic are "impossible." They know how to find a magical kingdom hidden behind a stand of old oaks, how to find the dragons under the ground. If we ask for their advice, they might just show us how to escape to the forest instead of building more towers.

21
Parzifal and the Fisher King

The Grail Overflows with Stories

Wolfram von Eschenbach's Parzifal is anything but a typical hero.[1] Strange, then, that von Eschenbach's thirteenth-century Grail epic romance about the wandering knight has become so foundational to interpretations of the hero's journey. Whenever I reread *Parzifal* I am struck by how much doesn't fit into a linear heroic mold. Detours are taken. Backstories are detailed to the point that they overwhelm the main events. The forest is entered and exited multiple times without a definitive symbolic initiation. Parzifal violates women and doesn't apologize. Characters wear giant ruby bubbles over their heads. Lances bleed real blood. Castles appear and disappear seemingly into thin air. Gawain's narrative interrupts Parzifal's, confusing the reader's attempt to "locate" a protagonist. If this is a hero's journey, then it is a failed journey that begins, steps backward, fails, starts again, and then explodes.

But what if this wasn't a hero's journey? What if it was a storyteller's journey instead?

The narrative seems simple enough. The wild boy Parzifal sets out to prove himself a knight worthy of the Round Table. But that's where predictability ends and creativity emerges.

Parzifal's first encounter with the Grail castle and the wounded Fisher King goes badly. Relying too heavily on other people's advice about correct conduct, he stays silent and does not ask any questions of the mysterious King Amfortas, who, according to von Eschenbach, "can neither lie nor walk . . . nor lie nor stand. [Who] leans, not sitting, in a sigh-laden mood." How can a king in possession of fabulous riches and the Grail itself be in such pain? Instead of finding out, Parzifal lets events play out in front of him. He "reads" the procession of lances, flowers, and beautiful maids without actually entering into the "text" of the castle and its symbolic complexities. He stays in his own story, abstracted by ideas about proper knighthood and duty. Later, flung from the Grail castle, he is admonished by his cousin Sigune, "Did you ask the question?"

Writing about the importance of questions in quests and fairy tales, Jungian psychologist and scholar Marie-Louise von Franz notes: "In itself, deliverance as the result of the right kind of question is a universal, i.e. an archetypal, motif. Indeed, in fairy-tales it is usual for the hero who wishes to acquire the treasure to have to fulfil one or more special conditions, on the correct execution of which the result depends."[2]

It is not until Parzifal's second invitation to the Grail castle that he enters into relationship with the Fisher King, finally asking, "What troubles you?"

Yes, the power of questions in myth and folklore has been the focus of much analysis. But it is not questioning but the nature of Parzifal's *specific* question that is crucial to this narrative.

This is not a question inspired by greed or the questioner's need to advance his own glory. And it is not a rhetorical question. Parzifal, who has asked for advice from multiple characters, both male and female, throughout von Eschenbach's romance, is not asking for more narrative direction. Instead, the question "What troubles you?" signals a profound shift in the character and a rupture in the text itself. The quest for the Grail pauses and dilates. Parzifal's inquiry seems to be the "flowering focus on a distinct infinity," as poet Lyn Hejinian describes it in her groundbreaking essay "The Rejection of Closure."[3] When Parzifal wonders about another being's experience, he opens up room in the romance for the real Grail: another story.

Parzifal escapes his monomyth and sheds any individual heroism. His curiosity and compassion open up space for another narrative. What is the cause of your suffering? How did this come to be? What does it feel like to be you?

Our educational system is defined by male narratives. People who are not white and male are taught to empathize with these stories. They are taught how to inhabit the stories of people who, in fact, will and have tried to silence, manipulate, and harm them. Literature and philosophy courses, almost always focused on male, white perspectives, invite non-white and non-male readers into the questioning role: "What is happening here? What troubles you?" Such an unbalanced education creates narrative malnourishment. But there is also a gift. It teaches two skills: how to empathically step into another being's experience and how to recognize that some people's stories remain silent because they are not asked for their stories.

In her memoir, *Recollections of My Nonexistence,* Rebecca Solnit writes:

> You should be yourself some of the time. You should be with people who are like you, who are facing what you're facing, who dream your dreams and fight your battles, who recognize you. And then, other times, you should be like people unlike yourself. Because there is a problem as well with those who spend too little time being anyone else; it stunts the imagination in which empathy takes root, that empathy that is a capacity to shape-shift and roam out of your sole self. One of the convenient afflictions of power is a lack of this imaginative extension. For many men it begins in early childhood, with almost exclusively being given stories with male protagonists.

It is undebatable that men need to get better at thinking like people and beings who are not men. This will not be hard work. I think, in fact, that it might be pleasurable. We might find that, like Parzifal, we heal our fellow "king," we achieve the Grail, and we inherit the castle.

As our capacity for empathy blooms, nourished by otherness, we will be able to see different narrative possibilities in our own lives.

But let us not mire the issue in gender. We are all bad at asking for stories. We live in a world teeming with narratives that we actively pave over and ignore every day. The Grail wasteland of our current day is not a physical location. It is our own malnourished ecological imagination. The Animate Everything is waiting to be asked for its stories. It's not that the dragonflies and the ivy and the fungus and the frogs and the mountain lions remain mute. It's that, high on our own narrative of human supremacy, we forget to ask, "What troubles you?"

Parzifal, when he finally asks the Fisher King for his story, has learned not what it means to be a hero, but what it means to be a storyteller. A storyteller needs a basket of stories. A multiplicity of tales suited for different seasons and audiences. A storyteller asks for stories, knowing each one will come in handy at some point.

It is fitting, finally, that Wolfram von Eschenbach's Grail is not a cup. Not a man-made object made for consumption. In all the earliest Romances, the Grail is actually a stone. What if the treasure you really wanted came from something you previously believed was inanimate and voiceless? What if it is a stone?

We must go to the stones in our lives and ask them for their stories. We must approach the landscape like a castle of marvels. Each bumblebee nestled in white lilac is the Grail. So are the vines sending green melodies up the sides of buildings. The mushrooms popping up out of the rain-plush soil. Curiosity and interrogative empathy will open up alternative worlds. We must turn to each other, arms open, ears pricked, and ask, with complete, rapt attention, "What troubles you?"

22

Sleeping Beauty, Sleeping World

The Prince Offers the Masculine a New Quest

The belief that the world is brute matter—automated, mindless chatter—is relatively recent. It dates back to the early sixteenth century when the rise of the concept of *sola ratio*—reason alone—began to divide science from faith and humans from an animate world.[1] Thinkers like Locke, Newton, Spinoza, and Descartes stressed "observable phenomena" as a new type of revelation. What we can see and prove, we can believe. While this paradigm shift could have bloomed into an increasingly sensual, interrogative mode of relating to the natural world, it withered into the bare tree of disembodied jargon and teleological excuses for using nature as a standing reserve of resources. Western philosophy has continually reified this dualism in its attempt to distinguish the human as different from every other flavor of being. Descartes gave us two things: a mind constituted by abstract thinking, and a dead world.[2]

But what if the world wasn't dead matter after all? What if, under the sloppy paint job of materialism and rationalism, the animate world was just asleep? Let us try to write a new Quest. A quest that surfaces in the fairy tale of Sleeping Beauty.

What can we learn from fairy tales and fairy-tale analysis? Fairy tales are a form of oral literature. In the nineteenth century the Grimm brothers collected tales from storytellers and set them to text. Likewise, seventeenth-century French author Charles Perrault, and even arguably Shakespeare, took well-known stories and set them to parchment.[3] They took breath-ensouled words, smoke-clotted voices, and gesturing hands and turned them into flat pages. This transformation isn't necessarily negative. At least the stories were preserved and widely shared. But it is important to remember that fairy tales were originally fluid, living narrative beings that changed to suit different ecosystems and social scenarios. A written text is more permanent, but it has a much harder time evolving. As Karen Armstrong explains in *The Lost Art of Scripture,* stories were originally somatic, lived, ritualized events rather than static, written objects. It was widely acknowledged that they would have to be updated constantly to suit the unique needs of a historical moment.

I mention this because the "original" texts of Sleeping Beauty, coming to us from Giambattista Basile in 1634 and, even earlier, from the fourteenth-century *Le Roman de Perceforest,* center around rape and abuse. But these are not the original stories. They are just the first written texts available to us, translated through male writers already deeply informed by hierarchical systems that profited from abusive power dynamics. Should we, then, not be allowed to step into the storyteller's role and "update" these stories for the present?

Charles Perrault's version offers an interesting take on the story. In it, the princess is put into an enchanted sleep in a castle with all of her other sleeping subjects: animal, human, and plant. A vast, entangled network of roses grows up around this castle, such that no one can enter. The scene recalls Eden, that first lost paradise, in this case protected not by an angel with a flaming sword but by vegetation itself, throwing up its thorns and vines and tantalizing blossoms. In Perrault's version the castle, overgrown for so long, becomes associated with ogres and dark spirits. Unafraid and curious, a daring prince manages through sheer force of desire to break through the enchanted briars. His curiosity and willingness to engage with the "darkness" melt away any difficulty. No dragons are fought. No blood is spilt. The castle "opens."

Eventually the prince finds his beautiful princess fast asleep in bed. Awestruck, he falls to his knees in joy. This is not the ogre he might have feared to encounter in such a place, or the darkness he willingly threw himself into. The outcome of the fairy tale is much sweeter and much more surprising. Sensing the arrival of her beloved, the princess wakes and exclaims, "Is it you, my prince?"

Instead of having the prince and princess make love or directly proceed to marriage, the Perrault version of the story, translated by Christopher Betts, gives us a wonderful alternative:

> The Prince, charmed with these words, and much more with the manner in which they were spoken, knew not how to show his joy and gratitude . . . They did weep more than talk—little eloquence, a great deal of love. He was more at a loss than she, and we need not wonder at it: she had time to think on what to say to him; for it is very probable (though history mentions nothing of it) that the good Fairy, during so long a sleep, had given her very agreeable dreams. In short, they talked four hours together, and yet they said not half what they had to say.

The picture drawn is of curious, enthusiastic discourse. The prince has come to ask the princess for her dreams, her thoughts, her ideas. They talk for "four hours," and it is implied their union will include more of the same. They share stories and longings and desires. And as they ask each other questions, stumble over the right words, and try desperately to communicate, the whole palace wakes up. Plants uncurl and flower. Horses neigh. Cats cast a drowsy eye at a mouse that had slept for a hundred years, nestled against its predator's sleek fur. Cooks, dozing in the kitchens, wake up and begin to prepare a sumptuous feast.

The quest of the prince in Sleeping Beauty is the quest of waking up the world. Sleeping Beauty isn't just a beautiful princess on silken cushions. Sleeping Beauty is the dry soil. The mites and fungi and invertebrates that enliven our lives without ever being noticed. Sleeping Beauty is the river down the road from our house. The elm trees, struggling against blight. The bees, winging chemical-addled flight patterns through pesticide-perfumed gardens.

Perhaps the prince shows us a new way of questing. What does it mean to wake up to the animacy of the world outside our front doors? It is important to be awake to climate change and to ecocide across the globe. But it is equally important to be awake to the immediate concerns of the ecosystem we specifically live inside. We can wake up to our local ecosystems simply and lovingly. We can go on nature walks and learn the names of native plants. We can find a bouncy hill of moss where we sit every day and watch the world, opening to surprising encounters. What different beings arrive? What weather blows across the trees with a vaporous story? As we wake to the stories and unruly voices of our intimate ecosystems, we can all take on a more serious role: the interpreter of dreams.

For that is the real magic of Sleeping Beauty. Beauty has been dreaming for a hundred years. She has been living in the mythic realm, receiving new stories and spells and rituals. The prince has come to receive these dreams, these stories. He releases them from their sleep along with the princess and brings them into active, waking movement. The plants, fungi, animals, stones, and landscapes around us do not have books. But they have dreams. And if we curiously enter into the thorns and thickets, we might begin to receive those non-anthropocentric dreams.

We have been living in the nightmare of reason long enough. The dead world offers no succor and no embrace when we confront the terrifying face of our misdeeds and violence. But, luckily enough, there are better dreams to be had. Outside our own heads. And they are the very texture of aliveness that constitutes our breath and the ground beneath our feet. Let us ask the briars and thorns and roses to give us better dreams. Let us take up the important role of sharing these new inhuman stories.

23

Melt the Sacred Masculine and the Divine Feminine into Divine Animacy

The Sacred Overflows the Human

Although I began my studies through the lens of the Divine Feminine, I find it is no longer big enough for me. The opposite of patriarchy is not matriarchy. The opposite of civilization is not an idealized return to Paleolithic hunting and gathering. The opposite of a human is not an animal or a rock or a blade of grass. The opposite of our current predicament—climate collapse, social unrest, extinction, mass migrations, solastalgia, genocide—is, in fact, the disintegration of opposites altogether.

Everything is both. And more. And everything is penetratingly, painfully, wildly alive.

Animacy is an overdetermined word, but so is the idea of the Divine Feminine. The reason I have begun to shy away from the Divine Feminine and the Sacred Masculine is their unfortunate identification with gender and, more importantly, their overidentification with humans and their myopic classifications generally. Animacy is plushier. Springier. More mosslike. It seems a soft spot to rest on while I try to understand and explain how very sentient the world is to me these days.

I am attracted to the constellations of meaning that sparkle like distant stars inside the word *anima:* breath, spirit, soul. And *animate:* to give vigor or life, to ensoul. I enjoy the animal itself, furred, horned, hoofed, clawed, scaled, and indeterminate, that bucks and bays and howls inside the word. I enjoy how philosophers try to clip it grammatically, like a twitchy nerve, and it keeps flinching away. It is a term I think most closely related to the original meaning of the word *spell:* the performative utterance. To summon magic. To myth. To story. To make happen. *Animacy* is the degree to which the referent of a noun is sentient. It is the "soul" that invigorates syntax with something very much beyond language.

Ultimately, I am a poet, and my choices often originate from a darker soil than common sense. Animacy, to my poet self, seems the "everything" of my actual lived ecosystem. The bright-blue darning needles weaving through thimbleweed and clover. The vultures wheeling through a hazy sky. The microbes in my gut, keeping me alive and nourished. The mycelium below my feet, holding the soil together.

The opposite of anthropocentrism is not any Divine Gender. The opposite of anthropocentrism is Everything. And what a tender beautiful thing it is to walk outside on a bright spring morning. Swathes of clementine light wash the pollen from the bricks of a nearby building. The robin's song is like the key turning in a lock. A handful of doves float down from the red-green cloud of a newly foliated maple tree. What a relief to realize that, unlike Adam and Eve, we haven't been severed from the Garden. The Everything still includes us.

The Everything is us, but it needs something in return. It needs us to melt our ideas of sentience as a purely human property. Or as a purely animal property. Or as a purely individual property. Relationships are sentient. Anima is the inhalation, carrying molecules and spores and pheromones into our bodies from the landscape. And then we exhale, sharing cells that have clung to our deepest cells, slept inside the pith of our blood. With every exhalation we decant ourselves back into the world.

How could we be one, or two, or three? We are more gerund than cold, hard noun. More animacy than strictly animal. We ensoul the world and are ensouled in return. Our myths about individuation and linearity no longer hold all the trouble. And all the love. We need to stop sticking out our two hands like it proves everything comes in oppositional dualisms. How many hands does the tree have? The peony? The pileated woodpecker? How many hands is the mycelium using to crochet intimacy from plant to tree to plant through the soil?

Divine Feminine just isn't big enough for all the relationships holding and constituting me these days. She thins my language into a one-to-one relationship. Even if she includes saints and "mother earth" and all women, it's easy to slip into the language of the singular. One mother. One relationship. One sacred gender expression. One temporality. One thinking animal. One species.

I'm not throwing her out, the Divine Feminine. I'm throwing her *in*. Melting her down. Mixing her into the messier, polytemporal animacy of everything I touch, change, and become.

The animate earth is a verb. An assemblage of verbs. A mycorrhizal system sewing together a whole forest. A shared breath. A midsummer celebration where everyone is invited.

24

Resurrect the Bridegroom

The Song of Songs and Ecology as Courtship

He that hath the bride is the bridegroom.

GOSPEL OF JOHN 3:29

Bridegroom is one of Jesus's most popular epithets, appearing more than fifteen times across the New Testament, and countless others in the Gnostic and apocryphal texts. Romanized Christianity, an invention out of pace with the Galilean magician by over a hundred years, misinterprets the bridegroom as the companion of the church.[1] But the Jewish people of Judea and Galilee would have felt a very different resonance when Jesus called himself the bridegroom. They would have thought immediately of the bridegroom of the Song of Songs.

The Song of Songs stands out in the Jewish scriptures. It has no truck with morality or law. It makes no great spiritual claims. The canticle's subject is love—impatient, erotic love—between a bridegroom and a bride. Composed orally around the sixth century BCE, the text is a green field, a practical Eden, dripping with honey and eroticism so thick and unruly it bursts open and outruns every metaphor employed by the author. "My beloved is a fawn . . . my beloved is a dove . . . a daffodil . . .

my beloved is like pomegranates . . . your hair is like a flock of goats." No one metaphor is enough to encompass the desire for the beloved. The metaphors tumble forward so fast that the effect is less of poetry and more of landscape streaming past on a drive through the countryside.

"Thy lips are like a thread of scarlet, and thy speech is comely: thy temples are like a piece of a pomegranate within thy locks. Thy neck is like the tower of David builded for an armoury," speaks one of the lovers (Song of Songs 4:3-4).

Bodies preoccupy the text, as does bodily desire. But each human body is porously participating in the sensual world. Breasts become fawns. Love becomes wine that becomes honey, then milk, then perfume, in an alchemical process so fluid we feel ourselves poured through the language into a love that is no longer bounded by the human. The bridegroom and bride open to a world that is actively opening to them.

This, I feel, is the realm described by Mel Y. Chen, professor of gender studies, in their book *Animacies*. This animacy Chen tells us, "activates new theoretical formations that trouble and undo stubborn binary systems of difference, including dynamism/stasis, life/death, subject/object, speech/nonspeech, human/animal, natural body/cyborg. . . . Animacy has the capacity to rewrite conditions of intimacy."[2] The landscape that the lovers of the Song of Songs inhabit is not a setting. It is a consanguinity. A participatory relationship that provides them with the language of love. It seems to actually "body" them. The bridegroom and the bride are less discrete individuals than they are holobionts: assemblages of relationships that constitute a greater whole. Cedars and daffodils and foxes and pomegranates.

No surprise, then, that the author never seeks to differentiate between voices. Sometimes we clearly hear the bride. Other times the bridegroom. And once, the brothers of the bride speak. "Take us the foxes, the little foxes, that spoil the vines: for our vines have tender grapes," we are told later in the canticle (Song of Songs 2:15). Who are the foxes? Does it even matter? They surface from the animacy of desire and then dive back in, demonstrating that what matters is less character and more aliveness—animacy itself pulsing through every cascading call and perfumed noun.

Lovemaking and animals. Beloveds so blended they remind me of symbiogenetic cells. As evolutionary biologist Lynn Margulis showed us, evolution is not always linear.[3] Major evolutionary events have been made possible not through a slow, steady trudge upward but through unpredictable partnerships and horizontal transfer of genes. It is through these complex relationships that our very cells came into being. What if we didn't need to *enter into* a sacred marriage? What if we already were one? Right down to the cells in a flake of dried skin. Contaminated intimacy at our very core. Lovemaking in every vibrating part.

I'm proposing a new sacred marriage: lichen. That mischievous symbiotic wedding of fungi and algae. At first the partnership seems simple enough. The fungi make sugar and the algal cells photosynthesize light. But the closer we look, the messier, and sexier, this union gets. This is not a marriage of equal opposites. It is a mixing bowl of multiplicities. This is no dualistic marriage of opposites. Lichen seems to be a fertile alternative to the old heterosexual *hieros gamos,* otherwise known as ritualistic sacred marriage.[4] How can we walk into more ecstatic, blended union with the world? We don't need seasonal sacred marriages to ensure the corn will grow. We need daily reminders that we are all mutually related and becoming. We need to slip loose our ideas of sex, our tired rituals of heteronormativity, and begin to dance with other species. Our cells are made of a love that is neither strictly penetrative nor gendered. It is lichenized.

The Song of Songs' shameless, enthusiastic eroticism stands in stark contrast to the rest of the Old Testament. Why, then, did the famous first-century scholar Rabbi Akiva state that while all of the sacred writings are holy, the Song of Songs is the "Holy of Holies"?

The Song of Songs offers us an alternative mode of masculinity. This is not the sexless, starved bridegroom of Christ's church. This is the man so consumed with love that he slips loose his edges and becomes every blade of grass. This is a bridegroom so rooted in his body, and the body of his lover, that he can't help but root down further, into the teeming animacy of the sensual world. Both bride and bridegroom mutually "build" each other from everything available. Each metaphor builds a lover by breaking down the human: erasing a cheek with a pomegranate, a pair of lips with lilies. Their love is a participatory, interwoven ecology. This a cosmogony as much as it is a love poem. Every drop of spikenard oil, every feather of the rock doves, builds a world.

This is the Jesus I want to resurrect. The man who knew the dense, vine-entangled love union he was summoning by calling himself the bridegroom. Jesus knew it was the holiest title of all. This is a man aware that courtship with the lover is really courtship with the whole, ecstatic, perfumed, chaotic landscape. This is the Jesus who told stories about mustard seeds and lilies. Who slept on the ground in the open air of Galilee.[5] What if we offered this new archetype to men? What would it look like to embody the bridegroom?

Let's liberate men from the lonely quest into the dark wood. Let's offer them courtship as a new mode of questing. Courtship as exploded from obsolete heteronormative rituals. What would it mean to go outside and begin to woo the trees? The foxes? The field? Let us acknowledge that the world is a green bride: playful, alive, resplendent, anticipatory. Waiting to be convinced into blooming by a song, an open hand, a bridegroom.

25

Osiris

The Original Green Man

"The fields laugh . . . the God's offering descends," reads one of the earliest references to the god Osiris in the Old Kingdom Pyramid Texts. Carved into stone, these texts date back to around 2300 BCE, planting Osiris in a world so far removed from ours that any attempt to enter it resembles a dreamer trying to recount a dream. Thankfully, the Egyptians were skilled artisans with a penchant for storytelling, monuments, and memorializing their rituals, thoughts, and funerary rites. Just as a constellation draws the stars into a larger picture, we can use these material fragments to constellate an image—a dream—of the vegetal god of the underworld.

We have numerous images of Osiris, painted on scrolls, etched into limestone, molded from gold and grass and mud.[1] In almost all of them he is depicted as green, wearing the feathered atef headdress that prefigures his hawk son Horus. His legs are often bound with mummy wrapping, firmly attaching his lower half to the underworld and the regenerative cycle of dirt and death. This fusion of legs echoes with older Paleolithic serpent gods and goddesses. His human form is emerging from the underworld and from the snakeskin of an older, less anthropocentric order of divinity. Osiris straddles elements and species. He is born of sky and dirt, with his father the land god Geb and his mother the sky goddess Nut. His child will be a bird.

Osiris holds the crook and flail. The crook represents his ability to work with animals, specifically sheep, while the flail will thresh the wheat. His responsibility both to the world of plants and to the world of animals literally "crosses his heart." He slips in and out of sober and systematic cultivation of fields and plants into the dreamier realm of ecstatic intoxication, introducing beer and fermentation to his people and traveling the world with his wife, Isis, to share his potent sacrament. His worship is associated with the *ba,* or soul. The word was associated with the ram and worship of the horned animal. Clearly, we have arrived at a more ancient version of the European vegetal figure known as the Green Man, wearing the horns that will later be inherited by gods like Dionysus, Cernunos, and Pan.

Unlike the vegetal gods that follow him, connected no doubt by a lively mycelium belowground, Osiris is not in control of the elements. No. He *is* the elements. He doesn't passively watch as the Nile floods the land, nourishing the soil. His body *is* the river, swelled by monsoons in the highlands of current-day Ethiopia, and withering into death and the underworld during seasons of drought. Modern-day myth analysis tells us that Osiris is a dying, resurrecting god. But it is more accurate to say that he is a thinning and thickening river, a seasonal manifestation. A riverine process that is rightly honored as divine.

And the Osirian river flows right into the fields, "making them laugh."[2] This short line, from more than four thousand years ago, is the potent green dream Osiris still offers us. The river is a god. The fields are alive. The god is less being and more relationship: water and soil mixing to make fertile loam. Yeasts and wheat and heat fermenting into sacrament. Sky and earth. Animal and plant.

In a version of the Osirian myth homologous to the current day, the green god arrives just at the moment when the sun god Ra has almost overheated the world to the point of death. Aided by the cunning of his powerful wife, Isis, Osiris manages to overcome the older god and offer his cooling waters to the baked land. We are living in a time of ecological entropy. The sun god Ra is our own addiction to progress.

We need, more than ever, the cooling waters of different stories. Osiris can teach us how to think like a river, how to think like an ecosystem of interconnection. We need to make decisions from the standpoint of relationships rather than the fictional idea of isolated species. As we think differently, pray differently, we might just be able to hear differently, too. Suddenly, one day, the river overflows, and the fields explode in laughter.

Unfortunately, after Osiris's initial vegetal celebration, his myth turns tragic. "O, sire, is this the waste? Unbelievably . . . drawn to the temple gate, O, sire, is this union at last?" asks poet H.D. in *Trilogy*, her transcendent meditation on Osiris and syncretism.[3] The tone is sorrowful, reminding us that Osiris is not the living king but the mourned and murdered beloved of Isis.

The myth goes that Osiris's brother Set was jealous of his power and devised an elaborate ruse to seize his throne. Hosting a party to honor Osiris, Set had a cedarwood box made specifically to fit his brother's dimensions. Playfully suggesting that whoever fit in the box must be truly divine, Set invited his guests to step into it one by one. When Osiris lay himself in Set's box, it was clearly a perfect fit. At that moment, however, Set and his henchman leapt forward, hacking the king to pieces. They closed the box and sent it out to sea.

The myth has many variations, the most complete of which are unreliably Romanized by Herodotus and Plutarch, but the short version says that Isis recovered her husband's body and managed, briefly, to resurrect him in the papyrean swamps, just long enough to copulate with him as she hovered above his body in the form of a kite. Set interfered again, chopping his brother's corpse into fourteen pieces, a fact that scholars have connected to the fourteen days of the waning moon, making Osiris a lunar king. The real magic happened when Isis, now pregnant with her bird son, Horus, alchemized her horror and grief by "planting" her husband's dismembered body parts across Egypt. Osiris's body, no longer king, became the kingdom itself.

There is an obvious invitation to men here. What is your box? What trap do you unwittingly step into again and again? Is it a myth about strength and stoicism? Is it a denial of heartache and complexity? Where do you benefit from systems of oppression? Where do you constrict your tender, expansive self to fit the mold of simplistic ideas of masculinity?

But I think Osiris has an even bigger, messier lesson for all of us: compost.

Veneration of the dead god was focused primarily on man-shaped garden vats called Osiris *vegetans,* where, yearly, priests would mulch soil, wheat, wine, spices, food, and plants for a month, ladling water into the sacred compost bin until a few stray seeds began to sprout from the "god." The compost god was venerated and then lovingly buried in a hillside or slipped into the river, completing the virtuous cycle of life and death, growth and decay.

Our ecosystems are constituted by constant cycles of growth and decay. Interruptions in this rhythm can have strange effects that highlight why life must always be balanced by decomposition.

During the Carboniferous period, nearly 360 million years ago, a bloom of early wood-based plants created huge deposits of dead vegetal matter that began to pile up without decomposing. Merlin Sheldrake explains in his captivating book on fungi, *Entangled Life,* that as these layers of dead wood accumulated, so much carbon was captured that carbon dioxide levels in the atmosphere dropped drastically, causing a global cooling event. The fossilized remains of these compacted layers of undigested matter are now the source of our worst friend: coal, the very substance fueling climate change today. Sheldrake hypothesizes that it wasn't until white rot fungus "learned" how to decompose and compost the deposits that the climate began to stabilize. The layers of undecayed coal represent a period of fungal absence.

This calls to mind Jesus. Unlike Osiris, Orpheus, and Dionysus, who will generously leave their dismembered bodies to compost into kingdoms, Jesus's disembodied resurrection removes him from the cycle of death and decay. Christianity and its malignant offspring, patriarchal capitalism, recall that fungal absence, those toxic layers of undigested matter. Fixated on ascension, Christianity forgets that you can't disappear the body. It has a habit of sticking around.

We are all struggling to step out of our boxes, individually and globally. Capitalism. Anthropocentrism. Patriarchy. Systems of hierarchy and domination. But, like our plastic forks and toxic runoff, this "waste" cannot just be thrown away. If we simply throw out what doesn't work, it will begin to build up and swamp us. We are already seeing the literal manifestation of this. Trash countries swim across the ocean. The air grows dense and confused with pollution. Throw-away culture doesn't work. Osiris teaches us how to plant the dead parts in the ground and how to make compost. How can we break down the toxicity?

Osiris invites us to do an inventory of beliefs. Where are our boxes? Where do we fit neatly into a paradigm that will ultimately kill us and all those we love? How can we begin to melt and mulch those patterns of behavior that keep us fitting within the rut of patriarchal capitalism?

Isis, gardener of her own husband's body, shows us that as we make compost, we also make love. Love as dirt. Love as vegetation. As H.D. suggests, that might be "union at last." The process of decay can be sexy. We can sprout new stories, new love, new growth, only if we surrender to the transformative magic of rot.

26

What's the Matter?

A Mycelial Interpretation of the Gospel of Mary Magdalene

"Will matter be destroyed or not?" begins the fragment of the Gnostic Gospel of Mary that comes to us in Sahidic Coptic.[1] And that is the question indeed. Is matter inherently evil? Does it represent the world of illusions? Should we strive to ascend out of it?

Modern Christianity is a sea of abstraction and guilt. But we often sense that there is a different Jesus behind the starved, dour martyr who comes to us translated through imperialism and patriarchy. A Jesus who, the Gospel of Thomas tells us, encourages marvel and a connection to our ecosystems.[2] What were Jesus's real teachings? What was this historical rabbi named Yeshua really like?

When the Dead Sea Scrolls and Nag Hammadi texts were finally translated and popularized by scholars like Elaine Pagels, it seemed that we were being offered a more authentic Jesus. Gnosticism, previously only understood through the tracts written by its detractors, was suddenly made directly available to us. We could read its texts and attempt to re-create the spiritual methodologies of its followers.

I, too, harbor a deep feeling that Gnostic texts, in particular the Gospel of Thomas, offer us a glimpse of the tricky, nature-based storytelling of the wandering magician Yeshua. They focus less on biblical prophecy and moral conformity and more on the highly subjective, interior experience of spiritual revelation. But there has always been a dissonance between the wily wisdom of Gnostic texts and their disavowal of matter, bodies, and earthly existence. The Gnostic cosmogony views us as "spirit sparks" that fell into a world of matter that continues to ensnare us in its falsities.[3]

Initially the Gnostic's disinterest in sin and repentance is refreshing, but it quickly rearticulates in the dichotomy of matter and spirit, of earthly illusions and illuminated understanding.

It is tempting to go back and massage these texts to fit our modern sensibility. We want them to encourage embodiment as well as teaching us how to kindle our inner divine spark. But it may be more useful, and more compassionate, to "stay with the trouble," to borrow Donna Haraway's concept once again. This is also what the Jesus of the Gospel of Thomas instructs us to do.

It is hard to locate exactly when Gnosticism emerged, but scholars, in particular James M. Robinson and Gershom Scholem, agree that it does not predate Christianity, and that it has early Christian origins. Others, including Pagels, hypothesize that it emerged directly after the destruction of the Second Temple in Jerusalem and the mass genocide of the Jewish people by the Romans at the end of the first century. This, to me, offers an explanation that resonates in my own flesh, my own "matter." A modern understanding of PTSD and somatics tells us that when someone experiences serious trauma, they often disassociate in order to survive. We cut our minds off from the suffering of our bodies as an escape mechanism. This instinctive response protects people who are undergoing unimaginable violence. But when it becomes embedded in the nervous system, the disconnect can cause physical and psychological distress.

Gnosticism, although fertile with spiritual insight, seems intimately informed by violence and the threat of obliteration. Jews were persecuted and killed by the Romans. Early Christians were also demonized and executed. And then, finally, the new Christian church, backed by Roman military force, systematically killed and erased any divergent Christian communities. Spirituality was intimately connected with physical suffering. The body and the material world were the source of great sorrow and great pain. The body could be captured, mutilated, and killed. Your holy temple had been sacked. The city itself had been burned to the ground. No wonder the Gnostics seek to ascend from a world that seems to only hold pain. They sought solace in a spirit so abstracted from the realm of the senses that it couldn't register the atrocities of everyday life. Will matter be destroyed or not?

What should we do with the Gnostic's aversion to the body? I want to offer a very Gnostic answer. Texts that represent a crystallized historical perspective will always trouble us. But spiritual texts grow ossified when they are not updated. We can't easily place a love of embodiment in the Gnostic worldview. But we can imagine a new type of Gnosticism, taking these ancient texts as inspiration. I want to offer a new interpretation of the Gnostic Gospel of Mary as a first attempt at updating a Gnostic perspective.

When Mary Magdalene asks Jesus about matter, he replies, "All nature, all formations, all creatures exist in and with one another, and they will be resolved again into their own roots. For the nature of matter is resolved into the roots of its own nature alone."[4] We can find parallels in the world of mycorrhizal communities, which connect and constitute trees, plants, and animals. For example, as forest ecologist Suzanne Simard explains, different mycelia infiltrate plant and tree root systems. Some mycorrhizae embrace the roots. Others slip inside the very cells of the roots. This seems a rooted way of imagining how "all creatures exist in and with one another." The underground hyphal network drinks in photosynthetic sugars from its symbiont (symbiotic partner) while also flowing nutrients, water, and carbon among trees, transmitting messages and warnings and "thinking" the very soil into biodiverse being. These fungal networks break down leaves and detritus, recycling nitrogen and minerals and carbon.[5]

From this perspective we can flip our anthropomorphic understanding of a tree. The woody, leaved parts could be seen as the legs and feet, while the tree's mind is delicately and dendritically rooted into mycorrhiza of the soil.

The Gnostic imperative is to go inward and to articulate our own specialized path toward enlightenment. Only then, at death, will we unite with the "monad" of oneness. But what if that monad was embodied and present all the time? What if it was the connective intelligence that constitutes the very ground we walk upon? In the Gospel of Mary, Mary Magdalene explains Jesus's teachings by saying, "He does not see through the soul nor through the spirit, but the mind that is between the two that is what sees the vision."[6] I read this as the intelligence of the interstitial. The connective tissue that thinks not through individuation but through a rejection of binaries, a celebration of continuity and collaboration. What if the monad was mycelium, breaking down life and then nourishing and building it back up again? When Jesus advises us to drop into the roots, we can take him literally.

His suggestion can be read as a kind of kaleidoscopic consciousness, popping in and out of other types of thinking. What is the divine spark of a tree like? The soil? The hyphal minds slipping in and out of root systems? We can be resolved into our roots and realize our roots connect to other roots, and still other roots, and still others . . . and on and on until our body isn't one localized brain but a sparkling gerund: connecting, melding, and becoming.

Why does God come among us? Jesus's answer is simple: God wants for every nature to be "restored to its roots." The importance is not in the mystical abstraction but in the very tactile reality of our embodiment in a specific time and a specific ecology. How can our spiritual investigations lead us into greater connection with the more-than-human world? When we meditate, let us not ascend, but descend.

I'm less interested in the soul these days. I'm much more interested in the dirt. So, I'm offering a new Gnostic maxim: Ensoulment is ensoilment. Soul is soil.

27

Knock upon Yourself

The High Priestess Wakes Up the Masculine

Step into the water, carefully, letting the temperature find the pattern of your veins. The chill, green current snakes up from the river, threading through the latticework of your capillaries. As you adjust, you step in deeper and deeper until, finally, you make the plunge, fully immersing. One last glance above, a smudged orb of sunlight hanging like spilled oil on the surface, and then you plunge into the underworld.

This is the realm of the High Priestess. Liquid. The tranquillity of aspen leaves flipped silver-side up before a thunderstorm. The dim, pearlescent swirl of lymph behind an ear or tucked into the soft skin of the groin. Secret. The body's inner water. The figure on the card wears a diadem and is framed by pomegranates, recalling her aboveground sister, the Empress. At her feet a crescent moon firmly roots her to cyclical time and seasonal momentum. Her hands rest lightly on a scroll labeled Tora, linking her to spiritual exegesis. As tarot scholars have noted, the letters can easily be switched to "Taro," linking the Jewish spiritual text to the world of the cards.[1] She sits between two Solomonic pillars, one white and one black, representing the dualities she acknowledges but does not embrace. She floats in the liminal—the watery connective tissue of relationships rather than the landlocked absolute of polarities.

The High Priestess, in most interpretations, stands for higher mysteries and intuition: the time of the dark new moon, when we must rely on our own inner sight to navigate. "Knock upon yourself as upon a door, and walk on yourself as on a straight road," advises one Gnostic text. "For if you walk upon that road, it is impossible for you to go astray. . . . Open the door for yourself, that you may know what is. Whatever you open for yourself, you will open."[2] The High Priestess always feels intensely Gnostic in that she is disenchanted with hierarchical religion and guru adoration. The High Priestess does not want us to outsource our intuition. She gently pushes us out of the temple, the church, the academy, and back into our own body. She says, "The only knowledge I have is that you know best how you should live."

The problem is that our culture teaches us to distrust ourselves. We no longer know how to identify healing plants, how to grow our own food, or how to build our own homes. We are told so consistently to work past physical pain and to ignore the "advice" of our own bodies that we are numb to the vital information our nervous and immune systems are trying to impart every day. When we ignore warning signs for long enough, they can manifest as physical disease.

Tarot cards, astrology, psychism, herbalism, and body work are typically viewed as "soft" or feminine. The dominant culture characterizes these practices as silly. But it is important to remember that this is only because the centuries-long Inquisition managed to eradicate whole populations of alternative healers and intuitives. It's easier to make fun of witches when all the witches are dead. Genocide has a habit of turning the instruments of the oppressed into a joke. Men are socialized by patriarchal capitalism to believe that anything that isn't strictly quantifiable, "scientific," or profitable can't possibly be helpful. They are trained again and again to outsource their feeling sense. Men are exiled from the very practices that could help them knock upon their own door and get in touch with their true vocations and self-expression.

But it isn't just the masculine that struggles to tap into real intuition. Modern intuitive practices have become pastel-colored social media campaigns. They offer advice on how to adjust to oppression by creating "peace" in your life. These practices are performed by clean, skinny women telling us to try harder and buy more crystals. This isn't about finding ourselves. This is about pretending we can buy ourselves.

Real intuition isn't one size fits all. And it isn't an inner voice. It is a door into greater participation with the landscape around us. It is the road beneath our feet that is also intimately a part of ourselves— including the dust and mold and mites and ticks. When we knock upon ourselves, we find that we don't exist in a digital vacuum. Our inner voice isn't so inner. It's a call and response with the world through our senses. Our inner voice is the bitter taste in our mouth, nudging us into an appetite for carminative greens that will prepare us for hotter weather. The indefinable smell of a lover perfectly suited to our microbiome and DNA. The cheerful sparkle of a finch across our path on a morning run, which reminds us of a similarly cheerful friend we should call and check up on.

The High Priestess is done with deracinated, capitalistic spiritual practices that prize the individual over relationships. She says that intuition isn't solitary work. No. It happens between the pillars of duality. It happens in the river that flows between landscapes, carrying debris and sediment and pollen. In the roots that work through soil, listening for the susurration of subterranean water.

The High Priestess invites the masculine to open to different ways of knowing. What would it look like to believe the sunlight had something to say? To believe the moon could teach us more about our emotional landscapes? She invites all of us to tap into the unique ways in which we connect to the world around us. What do we find beautiful? What invites us in? The plants and animals and smells and experiences we find attractive are like flowers drawing in pollinators. They attract us in order to teach us. The more we follow the path of our own curiosity, the more we will arrive at our real rooted intuition. We will find it blooming below an old chestnut. Sunning itself on a hot stone. Poking its green head up from black river silt. "Whatever you open for yourself, you will open."

We are not different from the environments we live inside. Our eyes, ears, mouths, and noses open into a world of sensual information that has the ability to feed and clothe and coax us into joy. As we open to the more-than-human world around us, it will send us back messages in our own voice. We will open. And then we will open.

28
The Kingdom of Astonishment

Gnostic Jesus and the Transformative Power of Awe

Seek and do not stop seeking until you find. When you find, you will be troubled. When you are troubled, you will marvel.

GOSPEL OF THOMAS

Seek trouble in order to marvel, instructs the Gnostic Jesus/Yeshua of the Gospel of Thomas, immediately signaling that this will not be the eschatological narrative of sin and redemption familiar from the New Testament. Our destination isn't the cross, ascension, or self-flagellation. No. Trouble is our vehicle and marvel—or astonishment, as it appears in other translations of the original Coptic—is our goal.

The Gospel of Thomas comes to us late but is arguably one of the earliest assemblages of Jesus's teachings. According to New Testament scholar Helmut Koester, the Jesus apothegms, formulated as a conversation with his disciples, may even predate the synoptic gospels of Mark,

Luke, and Matthew.[1] But due to the denouncement of Gnosticism and other "heretical" branches of Christianity in the early second century, these texts were lost to us until, in December 1945, a farmer named Muhammed al-Samman kicked open a red earthenware jar he had found in the desert and discovered the now famous Nag Hammadi manuscripts, containing among them the Gospel of Thomas. The work of scholars including Elaine Pagels has been integral in translating and synthesizing the fertile, textual landscape of the alternative modes of Christianity described in these manuscripts.

None of the Nag Hammadi texts offers a starker contrast to modern orthodoxy than the whimsical Jesus of the Gospel of Thomas. The entire gospel is bent on creating a sense of vertigo in the reader by virtue of doubling, paradox, and riddle. It begins in the first line when our narrator introduces himself as Didymos Judas Thomas, which roughly translates to the Twin, Judah, the Twin. *Thoma* (Thomas) means twin in Aramaic, and *Didymos* means twin in Greek. Twin is twinned. The voice of Jesus is nested inside a narrator already destabilized by doubling. The effect is less of confusion and more of dilation. We look at the page and characters double, triple, and bloom.

The Jesus of Thomas's gospel is constantly pulsing his teachings between union and solitude: "On the day when you were one, you became two. But when you became two, you became one."[2] But this is an easier saying as compared to "Blessings on the lion if a human eats it, making the lion human. Foul is the human if a lion eats it, making the lion human."

Scholars have noted that many of the maxims, although perplexing, relate to the life of a Galilean farmer and are similar to the parables of the New Testament. It is also interesting to note that the Gospel of Philip, another Nag Hammadi text, occurs in the same codex as the Gospel of Thomas and offers this famous passage concerning the relationship between Jesus and Mary Magdalene: "The companion of the savior is Mary Magdalene. But Christ loved her more than all the disciples and used to kiss her often on the mouth." Could it be, as scholars such as Harold Bloom and Elaine Pagels offer, that these trickier "stories" invite us into the more authentic teachings of the Galilean rabbi-magician?

Perhaps historical excavation is less interesting than inhabiting the marvel that the gospel repeatedly inspires in its reader. "I am not your master," Jesus reprimands the disciples. Instead, again and again, he tells them that kingdom has come already and is immediately present. "Know what is in front of your face," he quite simply advises. This is not the spiritually materialist mindfulness practiced by corporations seeking to improve employee productivity. This is not the sterile "peacefulness" that helps us better accommodate to oppression. No, this is ecstatic participation with the natural world. This is the interpenetrative experience of awe that occurs only when we realize the world is a polyphony of aliveness.

"Split a piece of wood. I am there. Lift up the stone and you will find me there," instructs Jesus. The "me" he speaks of is not himself but the kingdom of astonishment. The fragrant pith of the cedarwood entering our nostrils is the kingdom. The awe we feel at the moonlight-silvered grub under the stone is the secret gospel.

We live in a moment when we are woefully blind to the kingdom. Sensory gating, the neurological process of filtering out "redundant" stimuli from our sensual experience to create a homogenized reality, has been tightened by patriarchy and civilization. We quite literally do not see "what is in front of our faces."

Reading the miracle stories of older texts, we laugh at our ancestors' belief in "magic." But what if the magic is real? What if it is still here? As we codify expectations, we limit our ability to experience surprise and awe. In short, it gets harder and harder to change our minds and experience the marvel under a stone or in a piece of wood. We expect the ordinary and receive it in return, growing increasingly despondent each day, even when just beyond our blinders, mountains move and kingdoms explode from mustard seeds. Lucky that our brains are malleable. There are still methods of dilating into greater participation with the divine animacy of the natural world.

While there has lately been great excitement about the therapeutic effects of entheogens (mushrooms, LSD, hallucinogens), I think that it is important to stress that the psychedelic does not always have to be a substance intervention. It is not a heroic dose or an isolated experience. Functional MRI studies of the default mode network of brains demonstrate how entheogens work to shut off the "ego" centers of our brains; we have also shown that other exercises produce similar brain scans.[3]

I am talking, of course, about the practice Jesus offers at the start of the Gospel of Thomas. Overwhelming marvel. Astonishment. Awe. That dumbstruck laughter that lifts us up by the scruff of the neck like a mama cat transporting her kittens. These moments are not focused on the individual. They are always a participatory involvement with the world. With landscape and breath and weather. With flora and fauna and fungi. This, I think, is the most transformative psychedelic experience we can have: repeatedly flowing into the ecosystem and letting it flow back into us. Awe isn't the speedy experience of popping a tab or a pill. It's about going on the same walk every day. Sitting under the same black locust tree every morning. Slowly, quietly opening to what is in front of our face.

The messianic Jesus of the Romanized Gospels preaches dissatisfaction. The kingdom is always just beyond our grasp. But the tricky Jesus of the Gospel of Thomas says, "What you are looking for has come." The kingdom is always available, just beyond our sensory gating. The miracles aren't extinct. We just have to open enough to let them in. Then we spot the robin building her nest from eiderdown and string. Or the spotted salamander dancing across the rain-slick asphalt. We split a stone and find the kingdom. "Anything will give up its secrets if you love it enough" is a quote attributed to George Washington Carver. Thomas's Jesus teaches us that the key to the kingdom is our ability to center in our relationship to place, to the present moment, and to the sentience of the Animate Everything. The more we love, the more we see. Maybe then, troubled with love, melted into otherness, we will marvel.

29

Healing the Healer

Dionysus Rewilds Jesus

The kingdom of heaven is like to a grain of mustard seed,
which a man took, and sowed in his field: which indeed is
the least of all seeds: but when it is grown, it is the greatest
among herbs, and becometh a tree, so that the birds of the
air come and lodge in the branches thereof.

MATTHEW 13:31–32

Mustard greens were the bane of Galilean farmers.[1] They invaded crops, flooded fields, and crowded out grain. They overtook herb gardens. What is Jesus really saying in the parable above? The kingdom of heaven is as wily and tenacious as a weed. The kingdom of heaven is a process of rewilding. Look to his other parables, across the New Testament and the Gnostic texts, and you will see that Jesus's teachings are always ecological.

The parable of the sower is perplexing. But when we remove our anthropocentric filter, we understand that Jesus is explaining the wild, intuitive pollination of birds and animals, rather than systematic farming. Be like the lilies, the birds, the children! he tells us. Be passerby, be nobody, he says in the Gospel of Thomas. What a tragedy then, that this tricky Galilean magician gets remembered as a god of asceticism and death. Not only that, but we have forgotten the ecology of his homeland. Based on historical records and ecological research, Jesus's Galilee and much of Palestine was lush, richly vegetated, and densely flowered. Magdalene scholar Michael Haag describes it as most closely resembling the rolling countryside of Provence in France.[2]

A god of vegetation and wine miracles who declares, "I am the true vine"? Who does that remind you of? We need not jump down the rabbit hole of proving that Jesus was Dionysus.[3] We could just as easily say that he was Attis or Osiris or Orpheus. The truth is probably very simple: a historical Jewish rabbi with nature-based teachings made himself uniquely available to mythic interpretation, and the followers of Dionysus were primed to convert to Christianity. The relationship exists underground. There is no need to dig it up completely.

The Gospel of John bears a striking resemblance to Euripides's *Bacchae*. The wedding at Cana, where Jesus is said to have transformed water into wine, is a direct copy of the annual Dionysian miracles in the district of Ellis in ancient Greece, where stone vessels of water also transformed overnight into wine. English classicist A. D. Nock in *The Journal of Hellenic Studies* has shown definitively that the writers of the gospel seized an opportunity to paint Jesus as a new version of the older god. But how quickly Jesus is robbed of the traits that make Dionysus so fertile. The vine withers as soon as it is uprooted and nailed to the cross.

The minute Jesus's Aramaic oral teachings are translated and written down in the very language of the empire that put him to death, he is uprooted. Perhaps we can think of Jesus and Christianity today as a potted plant: anemic, rot-mottled, wrenched from a natural ecosystem that no longer exists. Of course his teachings are easily corrupted. They no longer have a root system tying them back into the mycelial and matrilineal matrix of a landscape that had lived in flowing communion with Judaism, literally accepting the mineral-rich bones of ancestors to make new soil, accepting the blood and food offerings of ritual, responding to farming hands and the psalm/song lines of generations dating back to the original grain agriculturalists, the Natufians.

Not only are Jesus's teachings deracinated by the language of his oppressors (Coptic and Greek), but he is denied that holiest of rites—interment and reintegration into the earth of his homeland. Jesus's resurrection is decidedly not a natural event. While Dionysus is dismembered and composted to regenerate the earth, Jesus is disembodied, leaving no corpse behind. His myth exits the virtuous cycle of decay, and thus exits the ability to understand and tend to nature. This is the key difference. The Gospels disembody Jesus, while Dionysus is primarily a god of embodiment.

I think now it is important not to prove an old relationship between the two gods but to foster a new one. Jesus has been divided from the ecology of his teaching for long enough. He was never planted in the ground he so loved, forced instead to evaporate into sterile celibacy. Let us ask Dionysus to give Jesus back his Galilee, his vine, his mustard seeds. Dionysus offers Jesus a drink of wine and asks him, not for spiritual advice, but for the stories of the flowers and animals and fish of his homeland that no longer exists. This healing could extend well beyond scripture.

Dionysus can teach men how to heal other men. He teaches men to ask how patriarchy has mistranslated their passions, hopes, and heartbreak. He invites them to go back to the raw wound where they were uprooted from the umbilical wisdom of their body's connection to matter/mother. This healing can be practical, giving men a language of nuance, tenderness, and dynamism about the ways in which they have misunderstood each other. And this language comes from the local.

That is the gift of Jesus/Rabbi Yeshua and his teachings. The parables spring from his homeland, his native ecology. Ultimately, the healing parables will not be ones from a distant land, strained through the metaphors of empire. They will be the rooted animacy just outside our door. The birdsongs that are intimately shaped to the open seashell of an ear.

Dionysus gives Jesus back his body. Jesus gives us back the local—the contaminated, interwoven complexity of the landscape we interpenetrate and become with each barefoot step, each completed breath.

30

Making Amends to Attis and Adonis

No Gods Were Killed in the Making of This Myth

Just because a myth is old doesn't mean it's healthy.

Did you know that the Christian Holy Week is directly layered on top of the celebration of the dying and resurrecting god Attis? And Adonis and Dumuzi and Tammuz . . .[1] The line of terminally wounded vegetal gods stretches back beyond written language, each one steeped in the last one's blood. Passion Week processions directly echo the procession of the *melissae,* or priestesses, of Cybele, strewing flowers and mourning the dead god Attis by parading around a pine tree wrapped in violets and ribbons.

It's easy to romanticize these stories. Adonis, born of a myrrh tree, the impossibly beautiful lover of the goddess Aphrodite, is fatally wounded by a boar. His hemorrhaging wound gives birth to the first bright red anemones. From tree to youth to flower. You could almost forget the rupture that draws in the fragrant, floral details like a black hole. The Phrygian god Attis's fate is similarly violent. Born of a river goddess, the beautiful youth is shamed by his goddess lover Cybele for falling in love with a human woman. He self-castrates and bleeds to death, becoming a tree, like Adonis, and giving birth to the first violets. Variations of this same story stretch back to Inanna and her sacrificed lover Dumuzi and to Astarte and Tammuz.

The classic mythological interpretation is that these dying, resurrecting gods represent the primordial rhythms of the seasons, the tides, and the moon.[2] The king must die. And then, assuredly, he will return—just as long as we do the right rituals and carry flowers through the streets. The apogee of this mythological trend is Jesus's crucifixion. A storytelling magician's murder is transformed into a commentary on the seasons and the necessity of suffering in order to experience spiritual transformation.

Myth analysis is often suffused with a yearning to locate and resurrect an early, "more natural" ecosystem of stories and beliefs. But as long as we depend on written culture, on sessile agricultural civilizations, the available myths will always come closely wedded to the abstraction of phonetic alphabets and the unfortunate side effects of agriculture: disease, overpopulation, misogyny, and war.

What if the dying, resurrecting god was not as natural a story as we've been led to believe? What if it didn't so easily echo with "the return of spring"? There seems to be something deeply naive about assuming that the god will resurrect. How many times can we gore a lover, send him to the underworld, castrate him, before he says, "Enough already. I don't want to come back."

What I want to say, loudly, forcefully, is this: It is only initiation if you survive. And many do not survive. The way we live produces suffering, both our own and the suffering of others. It is only natural that our myths have sought to justify this suffering as sacred initiation or the only grounds for rebirth and transformation. On a personal scale we defend our addictions with stories. On a larger scale we defend our addiction to violence with violent mythologies.

What if we looked at Attis and Adonis and Tammuz and Dumuzi as failed initiations? The end result of a fetishization of suffering and a deeply repressed guilt about living outside natural rhythms?

Myths about ritual sacrifice and rebirth have bled into our mythologies about the environment. You can clear-cut an old-growth forest and it will grow back. You can redirect a massive river and the land around it will bend and smooth. You can drive the bees into extinction and flowers will still return every spring. But it turns out, when you cut down mother trees and then plant a homogenized forest without a rhizomatic system belowground and biodiversity aboveground, your forests don't flourish and will smolder into forest fires. When you redirect a river, you interrupt the sediment buildup that stabilized coastal land. Louisiana, in this way, sinks deeper into the sea.[3] When will we wake up to the fact that resurrection is not a given?

When you kill Adonis, mostly he stays dead. When you destroy ecosystems, mostly they don't regenerate in a way that is green and easy and celebratory.

Just because a myth is old doesn't mean it's healthy. Just because a story has been told for four thousand years doesn't mean it can't be retold. A classic anthropocentrism suffuses these stories. We only "get" violets and trees and anemones because these humans died. We only get "forgiveness" because Jesus died for our sins.

What if the crucifixion was a mistake? What more could Jesus have learned and taught if he had lived past the tender age of thirty-three?

What if there was a world before words? Before wounded gods? A world full of pine trees and old-growth forests and violets and roses? A world where forgiveness was not something that we earned but as ubiquitous as air, inhuman and plentiful, tender and pleasurable, suffusing every day, every waking hour?

31

The Joyful Rescue

Tolkien's Eucatastrophe and the Anthropocene

As if to his eyes some sudden vision had been given, Gandalf stirred; and he turned, looking back north where the skies were pale and clear. Then he lifted up his hands and cried in a loud voice ringing above the din: The Eagles are coming! And many voices answered crying: The Eagles are coming! The Eagles are coming! The hosts of Mordor looked up and wondered what this sign might mean.

J. R. R. TOLKIEN, *THE RETURN OF THE KING*

Welcome to the eucatastrophe—the "good catastrophe" that Tolkien posited as the crucial ingredient in fairy tales and fantasy.[1] Death and failure seem likely. Everything is lost. And then, inexplicably, the impossible occurs and the consolation of a happy ending blooms like wild hollyhock in the aftermath of a forest fire. Tragedy, imminent just seconds before, melts away like (to quote again from *The Return of the King*) "a vast threatening hand, terrible but impotent: for . . . a great wind took it, and it was all blown away, and passed; and then a hush fell."

In this last book of Tolkien's Lord of the Rings series, Frodo and Sam have destroyed the ring but are stranded on the erupting Mount Doom. Just when salvation seems impossible, the eagles swoop down to their rescue. You'll recognize this trope in many of your favorite stories. Aslan charging in to save the battle for Narnia. Spiderman swinging in on his webbing to interrupt a robbery. The music, mournful cello strokes, quickens, alights, melts into flutes and horns and radiant wind. What makes a eucatastrophe different from deus ex machina (a literary trope defined as an unexpected event that saves a seemingly doomed situation) is that it plays by the logic of its world. It is both utterly impossible and totally expected, made even more poignant by the intimate understanding that actual catastrophe is the more likely outcome. The eucatastrophe is prayed for, imagined, "longed for," even as circumstances become increasingly dire.

Tolkien explained that, rather than upend the logic of the world, a eucatastrophe confirms the deep, natural order.

> I coined the word 'eucatastrophe': the sudden happy turn in a story which pierces you with a joy that brings tears. And I was there led to the view that it produces its peculiar effect because it is a sudden glimpse of Truth, your whole nature chained in material cause and effect, the chain of death, feels a sudden relief as if a major limb out of joint had suddenly snapped back. It perceives—if the story has literary 'truth' on the second plane . . . that this is indeed how things really do work in the Great World for which our nature is made.[2]

This is the greatest power of this "turn" of events. It doesn't rupture our sense of belonging in the world. This is no abstract ascension. Rather, the joyful turn embraces us, consoles our doubt in a caring, animate earth, and embeds us even more deeply in our lives, our narratives, our ecosystem.

This is the herbal medicine that cures an ailment. The stray cat arriving on our doorstep, jolting us out of a depressive episode.

The search party finding the lost hiker two weeks out, dehydrated, confused, but overcome with the rightness of rescue. Tears always accompany this shift. Tolkien describes this joy in his essay "On Fairy-stories" as "fleeting . . . beyond the walls of the world, poignant as grief."

Unfortunately, Tolkien blended his literary theory with Christianity, calling the Resurrection the greatest eucatastrophe of them all, neglecting the catastrophe that fanned out steadily from his favorite miracle. Tolkien ignores that Christ ascends out of the story. He isn't consoled. Or married. Or saved. And the Resurrection leaves behind a disaster that, like trash fires in northern Canadian waste islands, never stop burning, never stop generating, incinerating, and dispersing violence.

What if the mother, the wife, and the family of Jesus did not experience the crucifixion and resurrection as a eucatastrophe? The son, the brother, the husband does not come back to life. The evaporated, disembodied god ignores his earthly, intimate entanglements. In fact, it bypasses the suffering of the man on the cross to assume he didn't long to be saved like the prophets who came before him. Where was the Yahweh who parted the waters for Moses? Saved Daniel from the lion's den?

Expanding out of the anthropocentric world, imagine all those species that have not been saved from Mount Doom by golden eagles. The Sumatran rhino. The bleached coral reefs. The Catarina pupfish. The American chestnuts. The Midway noctuid moth. The story of extinction is not one of happy endings or joyful turns. It isn't even a story but rather a parataxis of expanding voids. If we are to entertain the eucatastrophe, we must hold the grief that infuses it with meaning—the much greater likelihood that no one is coming to save us. The fires are lit. The cross is built.

In the Anthropocene, an age that acknowledges that human forces work upon and radically and permanently change the chemical, geological, and biological composition of the world, it is not some malevolent Sauron who has orchestrated our tragedy. We have lit the fires. We have built the cross. We have forged the ring. The villain is ourselves. How then can we possibly hope for a favorable turn of events? At this point, do we even deserve a eucatastrophe?

The word *Anthropocene* attempts to locate a universal *anthropos,* "human being," and pretends that it is possible to evenly distribute the responsibility for ecological crises. This is inaccurate. There are hierarchical systems and governments that have created this crisis, and there are peoples bearing the direct burdens of these escalating catastrophes, entire countries that have had little to do with their orchestration. Feminists have critiqued historian Dipesh Chakrabarty's idea of humans as "force."[3] When we say humans are a "force," we risk fetishizing human beings' ability to change the very geology of Earth. In philosophical discussions of the Anthropocene, we often stand dumbstruck before the effects of our harm, amazed that we could be so powerful as a species as to have such a lithic effect. With each dry essay contesting geological epochs, another species fades away, another marsh is plugged in with concrete, another bird sings its last mating call out into a world that will never send back a mate.

So let me ask again, do we deserve a eucatastrophe? No. But as we acknowledge that human beings can and do make a catastrophic difference on Earth and on the survival of other human beings, why not create a joyful turn and make that difference eucatastrophic? This is not a call for techno-narcissism. The same thinking that got us into this problem will not solve the problem. Interferences that attempt to prolong the life span of extractive and exploitative practices will not bring tears to our eyes. They will not bring joy to the Animate Everything. They will not console. They will only, like Bilbo Baggins wearing the ring, draw out a half-life thinner and thinner until, like dissolving tissue paper, it barely amounts to survival at all.

We are not as individuals strictly responsible for the current state of ecological collapse. A tactic used by the real culprits—big business and oil—is to convince us that we, as consumers, are directly responsible and must change our recycling and shower habits to halt global warming. But that doesn't mean our actions are meaningless. We are neither totally responsible for our current climatological crisis nor totally blameless. This is a call to meditate on the small acts of eucatastrophe that we can enact in our own lives. Noticing a possum, hit by a car, still alive, and bringing it to a wildlife rehabilitator constitutes a eucatastrophe. Allowing a front lawn to run wild with milkweed and goldenrod and clover amounts to a eucatastrophe for struggling bee populations. Noticing that a friend isn't returning calls and stopping by to check on them is a eucatastrophe. Protecting old-growth forests from logging is a eucatastrophe.

The imperative in the Anthropocene, it seems to me, is not to long for our own happy ending but to try, day after day, in small ways, to give that joyful rescue to someone else. It's not about saving the world. This is not the "Good Samaritan" smugness of small deeds. This is the eagle swoop of radical interrelatedness. Intercorporality. This is the joy that acknowledges that tragedy still exists, still looms and is seeded in every decaying cell. Every small act embeds us in the dirt but does not preclude our ultimate extinction. Eucatastrophe isn't just a narrative tool. It is a way of creating intimate, dependent relationships with the natural world. No one is coming to save us. But everyone is coming to save everyone.

32

Sharing the Meal

Tom Bombadil Offers the Masculine Safe Haven

We find Tom Bombadil as a little-known, enigmatic character in Tolkien's Lord of the Rings series. Who is he? *The Silmarillion,* Tolkien's book about Middle Earth's mythological origins, has no answers. Peter Jackson conspicuously cut the curious figure from his films. Tolkien was noticeably evasive when asked to define Bombadil's role. Sometimes he said that Tom's character was based on a child's doll, another fantasy entirely, and that Bombadil was unimportant and should not be scrutinized. Sounding disgruntled, he once wrote, "Even in a mythical Age there must be some enigmas, as there always are. Tom Bombadil is one (intentionally)."[1] But just as soon as he'd refused to define Tom, he offered that Tom was "the spirit of vanishing landscapes in Oxfordshire and Berkshire."

What we know is that Tom saves the hobbits from the strangling roots of an animated willow using a song intimately keyed to the language of trees. We know from the first book in the Lord of the Rings series, *The Fellowship of the Ring,* that Tom is the "oldest of them all"—old enough to have seen the first raindrop and acorn. In Tolkien's universe, the world is created through song, and Tom, if we can define him as anything, is the last holdout of the original inhuman songs taught to the Ainur by Tolkien's god figure Ilúvatar.

In *The Fellowship of the Ring,* the hobbits ask Tom's wife, Goldberry, who Tom is. She tells them that he is master—master of the wood and the water and the hills, but without owning any of these elements. He honors and tends to the heterogeneity of the landscape, the teeming difference. His mastery is not characterized by domination, unlike the mastery that structures the rest of Middle Earth. His mastery predates elves and hobbits and wizards . . . and even acorns. It is the mastery of melody. The intimate ability to step into another being's particular song. When trying to explain her husband, Goldberry paints a picture of a man in ecstatic participation with his world, rather than a man trying to change and manipulate nature: he is "walking in the forest, wading in the water, leaping on the hill-tops under light and shadow. He has no fear. Tom Bombadil is master."

Tom's idea of mastery is playful, localized, and rooted. He shows no interest in leaving his forest. He respects his root systems, his rhizomatic connection to a very specific ecological assemblage of trees, ponies, rivers, and willows. Thus, when Bombadil puts on the ring, he does not disappear. Instead, it is the ring that disappears, neutralized by Tom's indifference to the fight over good and evil. Tom is chthonic, sedimented well before there were even roots or maple trees or nourishing rainstorms. He doesn't want a ring to rule them all. As Goldberry explains, to rule would be a burden to him. Tom lets everything belong to itself. That is his joy.

It is possible that the Lord of the Rings narrative is vitally nourished by the brief interlude with Tom Bombadil. Some critics say the episode diffuses narrative propulsion. But Tom, although he doesn't fight battles or perform wild acts of valor, offers something else. He offers a refuge from the temporality of man. He shows that there is always another mythology, older, slower, behind the fast-tempo stories of men. He offers the hobbits song. He teaches them to play. He refuses to deliver definite answers, stressing the importance of ambiguity and curiosity. He literally nourishes the weary travelers, inviting them to a table "all laden with yellow cream, honeycomb, and white bread and butter. Goldberry is waiting. Time enough for questions around the supper table."

The Shire is the hobbits' home. But it is a home that is entangled in the world of men and the time of men. It can and will fall prey to violence and domination. We all need another home, one that the philosopher Gaston Bachelard called the "primal hut of intimacy."[2] When we confront agony and harm, we survive by keeping the coals burning in the hearth of this primordial shelter: a promise that there is a safe haven that is immune to time. The succor of Bombadil's woodland and his home will glow inside the hobbits for the rest of the narrative. This is the Shire before the Shire. The song that watched all the other songs be born—that of the acorn, the rain, the elves, the hobbits. Some have hypothesized that Tom is Ilúvatar. But Tom would surely laugh at that name. At that huge responsibility. He doesn't make the world and teach the angels and elves and men to sing. He watches from an even greater, primordial distance. He is the audience of creation. In that sense, he is almost identified with the reader.

Tom's house is our house. It is a home outside of the story that provides safety from the story. It is a song that embraces all the other songs. As this exploration into alternative masculinities comes to a close, I want to offer something very soft, very tender. We are facing increasing chaos. Late-stage capitalism shows no sign of winding down. Even if we manage to cap carbon emissions, we have polluted and changed our environment to the extent that the effects will manifest for thousands of years to come. Climate change is already here, causing mass migrations of human beings and animals.

Like Tolkien's hobbits, we have a long, hard road ahead. We have friends by our sides. We have good stories to tell. But we also need to get in touch with that golden hearth inside ourselves that is not tied to progress and is not tied to one human lifetime. That part of us that remembers the first acorn and the first raindrop. That settles low, into the roots, when strong winds blow. This is the table within us that we set with wine and food and fresh flowers. People with wombs have an easier time imagining this inner sanctum—this "hut of intimacy." But the masculine has it too. The masculine is the master of the wood through celebratory, inclusive activity. He is the master of song and swimming and dancing and sharing his feast. The masculine can find shelter, alongside the hobbits, in the home of Tom Bombadil.

33

The Gardeners and the Seeds

Healing the Easter Wound

He wakes to the pungent smell of spikenard: wrenched roots. Sweat. Aloes and myrrh. Underneath these perfumes is a metallic smell of blood and urine. He feels a hard, cold tightness in his chest, as if he had swallowed a shard of ice. It is dark in the limestone womb. Something soft as a moth wing has been draped across his eyes. He feels he has forgotten something important.

It takes him a long time to remember he is dead. And that it was all for nothing. Never again will he see his little sister Yael and tuck a stray curl behind her ear. Never again will he stand on the shore of the Jordan, watching a kingfisher pierce the molten gold of the river's surface as the sun streams through the sycamores on the opposite embankment. Never again will he see his wife. Her keen eyes and wide mouth. Never again will he touch the papyrus-soft skin stretched across her collarbones. A series of foolish mistakes, an ill-timed trip, a misunderstanding and it is done. He had just begun teaching in earnest, had just felt his confidence poking up from the dirt like a green crocus nub.

Oh, if he could move, he would howl. He would tear his hair. He would scratch blood from his chest.

It is then that the noise sounds. Like thunder tearing off a mountaintop. A blue crescent appears, then fattens into the dim light of a full-moon night outside. A grunt and cheer. Men's voices. Someone laughs and then the light is blocked out as people stream into the tomb. Then the smell. Honey. Mead. Roses. Lavender. Wine.

"I need helping unwrapping him," a melodious voice, almost boyish, commands. And then he is being tossed by strong hands, pulled out of his shroud. Finally, someone puts their hands to his chest, pressing down, and he is awake. He is sitting up, able to stretch out his hands and legs and look through creamy lamplight at the group assembled around him.

They are an astonishing crowd. The man who leads them is tall and lanky, with long black curls, and naked except for a leopard pelt slung around his shoulders. Vines snake around his slender waist, and his lips are as red as the poppies just blushing across the Jerusalem hillside. Behind him a boy with auburn hair and wide green eyes smiles shyly, holding a lyre in front of his chest almost protectively. Two men, beautiful as girls, seem wounded. They are supporting each other. Is that blood running down the taller one's leg? And then, the strangest of them all, is a man with bull horns and a smooth blue face, eyes yellow and impassive.

"Here, drink. You'll need strength," the tall, long-haired leader commands, offering him a cup of wine. It is mixed with spices and shoots straight to his tailbone. Jesus, buoyed as if by hot air, slips from the stone slab and stands up. The young man with the lyre begins to sing and play with the liquidity of a river. He is crying as he plays, the tears as green as his eyes, snaking down his bare chest to the ground, where they immediately turn into rosemary sprigs. The men usher him from the tomb into the moon-hushed night. Jesus is weak. He can hardly walk. He wants to cry. To speak. But finds he can't. The leader puts a strong arm around his waist and helps him forward.

They walk away from Jerusalem, toward Bethany. Until they reach a field blue-black with freshly dug earth. It takes a moment for his eyes to adjust before Jesus sees that there are huge holes dug into the mud.

"Here. You're first," the tall man says to the bull-horned man. "A jar of honey for the lady of the spiral and a handful of apple seeds for an orchard." The bull-horned man knows what to do. He gently eases into the first hole. The leader pours wine in after him. A handful of anemones. Some seeds. Then the other men slowly, carefully, bury him. Jesus is shocked, but he adds a handful of wet dirt too, knowing for some inexplicable reason this is the most important thing he will ever do.

"Attis and Adonis, you're next. Pomegranates and mead. Wheat and wild roses." The two injured men are buried together, braided together with rose vines. And then it is the tearful musician's turn.

"Trees bent for lyres, leafed for music, will grow from you, Orpheus," the tall man says tenderly. He kisses the boy on the mouth once before helping him into the second-to-last hole. Orpheus pulls a string from his lyre and reaches up to Jesus, carefully winding the string around Jesus's wrist.

"It is time," the tall man says, gracefully sweeping his leopard skin from his shoulders and using it to line the inside of the final hole. He pours in the last of the wine and then climbs in, holding up a hand so that Jesus can join him.

Once in the hole, they curl into each other like twins in the womb. Jesus can smell woodsmoke and lavender in the man's shiny curls, can feel his hands pressing into his wounded palms. Rain is falling, washing the loose soil over their bodies.

"How long will it take for us to bloom again?" Jesus asks as they sink deeper into the earth. For a second the man's eyes are golden, like kernels of grain, and then the soil covers their heads.

"Oh, I expect it will be a long time. Thousands of years perhaps," Dionysus answers, and although Jesus can hardly hear him through the mud, he still hears the smile in his voice. "But when we come back, we won't be wounded or alone. We will flower all at once and make the entire earth a garden."

A FINAL BENEDICTION

May the moon blend us in the bowl of bothness.

May we compost our heartbreak, mulch our wounds, pour

water into the dry cracks of dead soil. May our wands

turn into snakes, our snakes to wands. Our swords to flowers.

May our pleasure be as intelligent and

revolutionary as ivy digesting a building.

May we find rain-water fermented mead

in beehives, gods surfacing, mushroom-headed

from the mycelial underworld. May we approach

mountains as our lovers, landscapes as our own bodies.

May we honor the porousness of our bodies, selves,

souls, breath. The place where our roots fuse

into other roots. The beings that constitute our song. The larger

song we sparkle in, as one small star in a constellation.

May our time be as slow as bluestone. As quick

as a hummingbird heart. As sweet as nectar. As thick as pollen.

As light as a spore on the wind. May we fill

the space left behind by blight, by extinction, by harm,

with song. May we heal each other. May we ask each being for its story.

Conclusion

A Cure for Narrative Dysbiosis

In my investigations into alternative masculinities, I've run up against a few popular personalities that raise my hackles. It seems obvious to me that their rhetoric about masculinity encourages violence against women and the environment. When these figures pop up in a discussion of masculinity, my immediate instinct is to outright denounce them; to work hard to show that their arguments are flabby and self-aggrandizing; to prove that their philosophical and psychological suggestions are inconsistent and ungrounded.

But, after much thought, much time in the mycelial rot-scape of Dionysus, Orpheus, Tristan, Merlin, and Tom Bombadil, I've had time to mellow. I'm slowly arriving at a different mode of engaging with these antagonistic figureheads of patriarchal masculinity. Instead of flying into a rage that is more likely to destroy me than it is to even touch them, why not operate from a place of curiosity?

Why do men like this take up so much space culturally? Why do their narratives catch on so quickly? Why do men whom I admire and love find themselves gravitating toward these controversial figures?

I have a working theory, and it doesn't start in my head. It starts in my gut. In 2010 I fell violently ill. Initially I was misdiagnosed with and inappropriately treated for parasites and Lyme disease. This involved more than twenty-four different courses of antibiotics, some of which were directly pumped into my heart via a PICC (catheter) line. It's well known that one course of antibiotics kills an infection while also, inadvertently, wiping out a good portion of your intestinal microflora. *Antibiotic* means, quite literally, "against life." The trick to recovering from antibiotic treatment is to dose with probiotics and fermented food directly afterward. Unfortunately, when you undergo course after course of antibiotics, punctuated by heavy steroids, while already seriously ill, it becomes almost impossible to rebuild a healthy microbiome.

The effect is nasty. The obliterated gut is left open to predation from pathogens. Following these treatments, I suffered constantly from opportunistic infections. Candida. Thrush. Bladder infections. Viruses. And then doctors would give me antifungals and more antibiotics, further exacerbating the problem until my intestinal lining was so shredded it could hardly absorb nutrients.

The simplistic idea of killing off the pathogens only left behind more open property for new pathogens in my gut. As more scientific literature was published about gut flora and health, I decided the idea of "killing off" the fungal and bacterial overgrowth was outdated. Killing these small beings only seemed to make them come back with more creative vitality, or worse, leave the door open for something nastier. The answer was counterintuitive. Rather than trying to kill these microbes, I needed to crowd them out with good bacteria. I needed probiotics, fermented foods, mushrooms, and even, I'll admit, finger pinches of actual dirt. The yeasts and bad parasites were only powerful and dangerous when they had free rein. They needed less space to thrive. As you repopulate a gut with healthy bacteria, they regulate the overgrowth of pathogens and protect you from parasites. A polyphony of microbial voices drowns out the monologue of a nasty pathogen.

Modern masculinity is suffering from narrative dysbiosis. I want to suggest that patriarchal masculinity has acted like an overprescription of antibiotics, effectively killing off healthier, more magical modes of the masculine so regularly that it has become difficult for them to grow back. What has been left behind culturally is similar to my scorched gut. Too much empty real estate. No wonder problematic figures bloom like candida. They don't have any competition. They are harmful only in that they have too much free space to grow.

So I am not surprised that so many intelligent, curious men find themselves listening to and reading the work of these fungal over-growths. They aren't presented with enough compelling alternatives. Confronted by the toxicity of the patriarchal masculinity, they search for something else. Anything else. I am sympathetic with their heart-ache and their questing. Where are the healthy stories? Where are the compassionate, fertile masculinities?

I am changing my tune. I don't think it's helpful to try to erase or "kill off" these problematic figures. They only come back stronger, sapping us of our strength as we try again and again to disprove their faulty logic. Instead, I want to overwhelm them. I want to crowd them into a very small corner of the cultural gut. I want to invite not one or two charismatic storytellers to the table. I want a hundred options. I want a biodiversity of masculinities. A polyphony of alternative nar-ratives. We can't cancel these guys entirely. But we also shouldn't give them a podium or twenty minutes of uninterrupted TED Talk time. Rather, let us invite them into a room with twenty, thirty, forty other charismatic artists and thinkers and storytellers of the masculine. Let us invite them into a healthy microbiome that makes sure they aren't allowed the space to overgrow their bounds.

Now, here, let me fall silent, stop writing, and start to listen. I invite you to share your own myths. Your own fertile stories. This book has been a monologue longing to become a dialogue, and then, hopefully, a polyphony.

Acknowledgments

Thank you to my family. Thank you to my parents, Perdita Finn and Clark Strand, for your magical and practical support. Thank you to my brother, Jonah Strand. Thank you to my oldest friends, my cousins Daniel and Adam Finn. Thank you to my animal kin: Fujiyama, Sputnick, Rosamund, and Oliver.

Thank you to the friends who supported, celebrated, and inspired me during the intense season I spent writing this book: Mary Evelyn Pritchard, Emily Rose Theobald, Marion Albers, Edith Lerner, Ilana Silber, Harper Cowan (and Poppy), Shea Settini, and Fiona Saxman. Thank you to Luke Otwell for holding down the fort. Thank you to Abbe Aronson and my French bulldog muse Tugboat. A very deep and special thank-you to Hannah Sparaganah for the mirth, for the conversation, and for never turning down an invitation to the underworld.

Thank you to the tarot deck that guided me through my own version of Tristan's night sea journey.

The Flowering Wand began as a short essay I shared on social media and quickly, within the space of a month, ballooned into a book with a devoted, supportive community of readers and collaborators. I wish I could thank each and every one of you, but if I did the acknowledgments would truly be as long as the book itself. In particular, I extend deep gratitude to Rafael Alvarez, Jana Astanov, Leah Baer, Sabin Bailey, Carrie Bills, Juliet Blake, Melea Britt, Polly Paton Brown, Katharine Burke,

Caroline Casey, Suzette Clough, Nicola Coombe, Liliana DeGiorgio, Maria De Los Angeles, Patrick Dodson, Cathy French, Jennifer Gandia, Rene Janiece, Meg Johnson, Mary Porter Kerns, Erica Klein, David Levine, Ian Mackenzie, Clayton Masterson, Betz McKeown, Leah McNatt, Karen Morrissey, Averi Ohman, Mat Osmond, Cathy Stevens Pratt, Clifford Rames, Carole Ribner, Diana Rowan Rockefeller, Miriam Ropschitz, Kelly Sophia Rose, Kimberly Saward, Daniel Schneider, Josh Schrei, Finn Schubert, Bee Scolnick, Emily Simpson, Camellia Stadts, Michael Steward, Matthew Stillman, Carole Taylor, Jane Lillian Vance, Robert Burke Warren, and Pamela Clare Wylie Samuelson.

A juicy, floral, delicious thank-you to Emily Shurr.

Thank you to Ann Lauterbach for your mentorship and guidance. Thank you to Robert Weston for teaching me how to read critically and encouraging me to turn my final college paper into an experiment titled "You Are in a Rhizome with This Text." It could be said that it was my first fungal foray.

A deep-rooted thanks to my editor, Richard Grossinger, for believing in this manuscript and coaxing a few last blossoms out of the ground. Thank you to Lyz Perry for your fine editorial guidance. And to everyone at Inner Traditions, including Manzanita Carpenter, Nancy Ringer, Erica Robinson, and the wonderful design team that dreamed up the cover with me.

Thank you to my fierce and canny agent, Anne Marie O'Farrell, for the laughter, for the wisdom, and for recognizing me, early on, as a writer.

I always write with musical accompaniment. *The Flowering Wand* exists thanks to the music of Dorothy Ashby, Emahoy Tsegué-Maryam Guèbrou, Sam Lee, Hailu Mergia, Angel Olsen, Hans-Joachim Roedelius, Nina Simone, and a healthy dose of disco.

Thank you to the memory of those men who taught me that masculinity is a multiplicity of tenderness and mischief: Leith Rogovin, Killian Mansfield, Noam Seligman, Dave Chandler, Jeff Jacobson, and Sebastian the gray cat. You all felt very close during the writing of this book. Dancing in the rhizomes right below my feet.

Thank you to the land that nourished, supported, taught, and directed me as I envisioned and produced this book: the Hudson Valley. Thank you to the Hudson River and the Rondout Creek. Thank you to Guardian Mountain and Overlook Mountain. The eagles, herons, hawks, ducks, and doves. The black locusts and mustard greens. Thank you to ghost pipe and reishi. The rattlesnakes and racoons. Thank you to Lewis Hollow and the stone cairns. Thank you to Cooper Lake and the Millstream. Thank you to the fungi and the birds and the beasts. Thank you to the albino deer. Thank you to the woodchucks of Cornell Park. Thank you to the Tivoli Bays. And thank you to the Munsee Lenape people, whose stories still surface with the mushrooms after it rains.

Lastly, and most importantly, thank you to Dionysus. Life has been much stranger since I invited you inside.

Notes

INTRODUCTION:
THE SWORD OR THE WAND

1. See, for example, "Apotropiac Wands of the Middle Kingdom" by Diane Leeman.

2. The origin of plant roots in relationship to fungi is explained at length in the book *Entangled Life,* by Merlin Sheldrake; the article "The Origin and Early Evolution of Roots," by Paul Kenrick and Christine Strullu-Derrien; and the study "Coevolution of Roots and Mycorrhizas of Land Plants," by Mark C. Brundrett.

3. The phrase *more-than-human* was coined by magician-philosopher David Abram in his groundbreaking 1996 book, *The Spell of the Sensuous.* Abram almost single-handedly laid the groundwork for the new study of ecopsychology, synthesizing philosophy, Indigenous wisdom, experience as a street magician, and his mentorship with both animals and shamans the world over.

4. These lines come from Robert Bringhurst's 2008 book, *Everywhere Being Is Dancing* (page 64). Bringhurst is a poet and interdisciplinary scholar of Indigenous language and folklore, typography, philosophy, and ecology. His writings about living in an age of environmental collapse have informed modern formulations of deep ecology.

5. See, again, Bringhurst's *Everywhere Being Is Dancing* (page 65).

6. Ethnobotanist and scholar Enrique Salmón draws from Indigenous

knowledge and land practices to articulate an ecology of kinship systems in his 2000 paper, "Kincentric Ecology: Indigenous Perceptions of the Human Nature." Salmón's follow-up book, *Iwigara: The Kinship of Plants and People,* is a practical guide to fostering kinship with native North American plant allies.

1. SKY, STORM, AND SPORE: WHERE DO GODS COME FROM?

1. For a more developed study of mushrooms, spores, and rain production, read "Mushrooms as Rainmakers: How Spores Act as Nuclei for Raindrops," by Maribeth O. Hassett, Marl W. F. Fischer, and Nicholas P. Money.

2. Mycologist Paul Stamets explains bellistospory, or mushroom sporulation, at length in his 2005 book, *Mycelium Running: How Mushrooms Can Help Save the World.* Stamets references the work of mycologist David Arora, who estimated that the single species *Ganoderma applanatum* could release thirty billion spores a day, and upward of five trillion a year. It is important to note that not all mushrooms produce an abundance of spores. Some are more conservative in their spore liberation, like the chanterelle, which paces the release of spores for up to a month.

3. These experiments are explained in detail in M. O. Hassett, M. W. F. Fischer, and N. P. Money, "Mushrooms as Rainmakers: How Spores Act as Nuclei for Raindrops."

4. Rajiv Malhotra is an American Hindutva activist and author. For more information, see his work entitled *Indra's Net: Defending Hinduism's Philosophical Unity.*

2. THE HANGED MAN IS THE ROOTED ONE: THINKING FROM THE FEET

1. The idea of the "root brain" was proposed by Charles Darwin in the latter half of his life. With the help of his son Frances, Darwin published a study on vegetal life titled *The Power of Movement in Plants,* in which he hypothesized: "It is hardly an exaggeration to say that the tip of the radicle thus endowed [with sensitivity], and having the power of directing the movements of the adjoining parts, acts like the brain

of one of the lower animals; the brain being seated within the anterior end of the body, receiving impressions from the sense-organs, and directing the several movements."

3. BETWEEN NAMING AND THE UNKNOWN: SHAKESPEARE'S *TWELFTH NIGHT*

1. The historical and political context of Genesis's composition is explained in detail by scholar Elaine Pagels in *Adam, Eve, and the Serpent.* Karen Armstrong traces the transition of oral Judaism to a textual tradition in her book *The Lost Art of Scripture.* For a developed history of the Jewish scriptures, I suggest historian Simon Schama's *The Story of the Jews: Finding the Words.*

4. THE MINOTAUR DANCES THE MASCULINE BACK INTO THE MILKY WAY: MYTHS NEED TO MOVE

1. The direct relationship between the Tehom of Genesis and the Tiamat of the *Enuma Elish* is recognized by many scholars. A. E. Whatham documented the textual and historical evidence of the connection in his 1910 essay "The Yahweh-Tehom Myth."

2. Joseph Campbell popularized the theory that lunar goddess culture was subjugated by northern solar heroes in his series on myth and comparative religion, The Masks of God. For a feminist analysis of the movement from late Bronze Age culture to Iron Age monotheism, I recommend *The Myth of the Goddess: Evolution of an Image,* by Anne Baring and Jules Cashford.

3. Carl Kerényi's comprehensive study, *Dionysos: Archetypal Image of Indestructible Life,* begins with a thorough analysis of Minoan history and Minotaur mythology. The bull god archetype is also discussed at length in *The Myth of the Goddess* mentioned above.

4. Riane Eisler provides an excellent analysis of Cretan archaeological evidence in her seminal book, *The Chalice and the Blade.*

5. Some of the earliest images of mother goddesses, painted or carved into stone during the early Neolithic period, pair her with snakes or make her form distinctly serpentine. Chapter 1 of Baring and Cashford's *The Myth*

of the Goddess, titled "In the Beginning: The Paleolithic Mother Goddess," presents archaeological evidence and analysis of this iconographic trend.

6. Drawing on Grave's work, Campbell develops this argument in vol. 3 of The Masks of God. He argues that the historical thirteenth-century BCE invasions are rearticulated mythically in figures such as Medusa and Perseus.

7. In Dionysos, Carl Kerényi shows that the bull monster was, in all likelihood, a bull god revered in connection to astronomical events such as comets and meteors.

8. A study of the Linear B tablets can be found in the article by A. P. Judson "The Mystery of the Mycenaean 'Labyrinth'" included in *SMEA NS* 3, pages 53–72.

5. THE MOON BELONGS TO EVERYONE: LUNAR MEDICINE FOR THE MASCULINE

1. The phrase "God is change" originates in Butler's apocalyptic science-fiction novel *Parable of the Sower.*

6. BECOMING A HOME: THE EMPRESS CARD EMBRACES THE MASCULINE

1. For a comprehensive analysis of imagery in the tarot's Major Arcana, I suggest the book *Seventy-Eight Degrees of Wisdom: A Tarot Journey to Self-Awareness,* by Rachel Pollack.

2. Pitcher plants and their hosted communities are explained by ecologist Matt Candeias in his book, *In Defense of Plants.* For an in-depth investigation of inquiline communities in bromeliads, see the 2020 study by K. J. Gilbert et al., "Tropical Pitcher Plants (Nepenthes) Act as Ecological Filters by Altering Properties of Their Fluid Microenvironments."

7. DIONYSUS: GIRL-FACED GOD OF THE SWARM, THE HIVE, THE VINE, AND THE EMERGENT MIND

1. For a complete collection of primary sources and texts about Dionysus and the Greek pantheon, read *Anthology of Classical Myth: Primary*

Sources in Translation, compiled by Stephen M. Trzaskoma, R. Scott Smith, and Stephen Brunet. Additionally, Carl Kerényi offers an anthropological and poetic analysis of primary sources in *Dionysos: Archetypal Image of Indestructible Life.*

2. The mythological origins of Semele are discussed by Bronze Age specialist Marija Gimbutas in her book, *The Living Goddesses.* Linguists debate whether Semele derives from the Proto-Indo-European word for "earth." It is interesting to note that *seme* means "seed" in current Slavic languages. In his 2014 article "Non-Iranian Origin of the Eastern-Slavonic God Xŭrsŭ/Xors," professor of linguistics Constantine Borissoff suggests that Semele could be "an important link bridging the ancient Thracian and Slavonic cults."

3. Dionysus is famously enshrined in the classical Athenian tragedy *Bacchae,* by Euripides. Many of our ideas about his physicality and demeanor derive from the long-standing popularity of this gruesome drama.

4. There has been fascinating research into the specific beverages consumed by the followers of Dionysus. A recent book, *The Immortality Key,* by Brian Muraresku, explores the connection between Paleolithic graveyard beers, the Eleusinian mysteries, and the cult of Dionysus.

5. A helpful explanation of the immune benefits of mushrooms can be found in the 2014 study "Immune Modulation from Five Major Mushrooms: Application to Integrative Oncology," by Alena G. Guggenheim, Kirsten M. Wright, and Heather L. Zwickey.

8. MERLIN MAKES KIN TO MAKE KINGDOMS: A MULTIPLICITY OF MINDS AND MYTHS

1. Eleventh-century British cleric Geoffrey of Monmouth is regarded as initiating British historiography. His histories, full of dragons and magic, read to us less as historical and more as fiction. Composing his histories, Geoffrey used an amalgamation of myth, folklore, and annals. Scholar Nikolai Tolstoy, in his book *The Quest for Merlin,* suggests that we can credit Geoffrey with creating the character of Merlin out of an assortment of different historical and mythic figures.

2. The Welsh poem dates back to the thirteenth century and is found in the Mabinogion, a fourteenth-century manuscript compiling earlier oral Welsh traditions. While the author is anonymous, the poem has traditionally been associated with the bard Taliesin and his counterpart Merlin.

3. The concept of culpability, paraphrased in Donna Haraway's *Staying with the Trouble,* originates in Belgian philosopher of science Isabelle Stengers' book *Cosmopolitics I.* Stengers argues for an "ecology of practices" where science (and other epistemological projects) are defined not by polemics but by overlapping interdependence. We can expand this idea to our own lives. We need to work across species, across beliefs, to honor and develop our connections with our ecosystems.

9. JOSEPH, SECRET VEGETALISTA OF GENESIS: PLANTS USE MEN TO DREAM

1. Rabbi Joseph Telushkin provides a thorough analysis of the Joseph narrative in his 2002 book *Biblical Literacy,* combining scriptural exegesis with midrash traditions.

2. These lines come from Dale Pendell's controversial 1995 work *Pharmako/Poeia,* in which he combines his ethnobotanical knowledge with a flair for dangerous experiments, documenting and investigating plants and substances normally classified as poisonous.

3. An overview of Neolithic dream incubation sites can be found in the comprehensive feminist history *The Great Cosmic Mother,* by Monica Sjöö and Barbara Mor.

4. Professor of religion and Jewish studies Mark Leuchter has identified the language used in the Joseph narrative as Classical Hebrew, sometimes called Biblical Hebrew, dating its composition to the monarchic period in the eighth century BCE. This suggests, however, that the story was already orally popular at that time—which would mean that the historical events it records occurred much earlier. For more information, see Leuchter's 2013 article "Genesis 38 in Social and Historical Perspective." And for a further exploration of the historicity of the Joseph narrative, read Professor

Israel Knohl's 2019 article "Joseph and the Famine: The Story's Origins in Egyptian History."

10. ACTAEON IS THE KING OF THE BEASTS: FROM CURSE TO CROWN

1. The relationship between Actaeon and Gilgamesh is noted by Michael C. Astour in his 1965 book, *Hellenosemitica: An Ethnic and Cultural Study of West Semitic Impact on Mycenaean Greece.*
2. For an overview of goddesses and their consorts, see chapter 4, "The Bronze Age: Mother Goddess and Her Son-Lover," in *The Myth of the Goddess,* by Anne Baring and Jules Cashford.
3. Author Barbara Ehrenreich writes about cave art's lack of human forms in a 2019 article for *The Guardian* titled "'Humans Were Not Centre Stage': How Ancient Cave Art Puts Us in Our Place."
4. This quotation comes from Anne Carson's translation of Euripides's *Bacchae,* titled *Bakkhai.*

11. A NEW MYTH FOR NARCISSUS: SEEING OURSELVES IN THE ECOSYSTEM

1. This observation comes from John Berger's book *Ways of Seeing,* which was based on his BBC television program of the same name. His work supported feminist interpretations of the depiction of women in art and popular culture.

12. EVERYONE IS ORPHEUS: SINGING FOR OTHER SPECIES

1. Both Anne Baring's work with Jules Cashford in *The Myth of the Goddess* and Joseph Campbell's The Masks of God series document the agricultural and vegetal themes that accompany dying and resurrecting gods.
2. For more details on honey fungus *(Armillaria ostoyae)* in Malheur National Forest, including the Humongous Fungus, as the reporting foresters call it, see *The Malheur National Forest: Location of the World's Largest Living Organism [The Humongous Fungus],* by Craig L. Schmitt and Michael L. Tatum.

3. For a better understanding of underground mycelial networks, see Merlin Sheldrake's *Entangled Life*. For a phytocentric (tree-focused) perspective, see forest ecologist Suzanne Simard's memoir *Finding the Mother Tree*.

4. Native to Hawaii, the last surviving Kaua'i 'ō'ō male was recorded for the Cornell Lab of Ornithology. He died in 1987.

5. The neologism *solastalgia* was created by environmental philosopher Glenn Albrecht during his study of the emotional impact of persistent drought in a rural area of New South Wales. He proposed this new term in his 2007 essay "Solastalgia: The Distress Caused by Environmental Change."

6. Multispecies feminist theorist Donna Haraway offers "making kin" as a way to navigate the chaos of climate change and ecocide. Haraway "troubles" the idea of the Anthropocene and highlights the entangled complexity of human relationships with the animal, plant, and fungal worlds.

13. DIONYSUS AS LIBER:
THE VINE IS THE
TOOL OF THE OPPRESSED

1. Dionysus's declaration is found in the early pages of Euripides's *The Bacchae*, as translated by Gilbert Murray.

2. Ovid memorializes the many names of Dionysus in book 4 of *Metamorphoses*, ending with an invocation of his role as Liber: "[The Boiotian bacchantes] called on Bacchus [Dionysus] by his many noble names: Lyaeus, Bromius; child of flaming fire; alone twice mothered and alone twice born; great lord and planter of the genial grape; Nyseus too, and Lenaeus and Thyoneus, whose locks are never shorn; Nyctelius, Iacchus, Euhan, father Eleleus; and all the countless titles that are yours, Liber, throughout the lands of Greece."

3. Information about Spartacus's unnamed wife comes to us by way of Plutarch, a first-century Greek philosopher and historian. He noted: "It is said that when he [Spartacus] was first brought to Rome to be sold, a serpent was seen coiled about his face as he slept, and his wife, who was of the same tribe as Spartacus, a prophetess, and subject to visitations of the Dionysiac frenzy, declared it the sign of a great

and formidable power which would attend him to fortunate issue. The woman shared in his escape and then lived with him" (Plutarch, *Crassus.* 9.3).

4. The Senatus Consultum de Bacchanalibus (Senatorial Decree Concerning the Bacchanalia), an engraved bronze tablet dating to around 186 BCE, details the prohibition against Dionysus and his followers after the Punic War and the uprising of Paculla Annia. However, historians agree that covert Dionysian practices persisted for many years following the ban, eventually merging into proto-Christian communities. For a full historical overview of the revolt, consult *Conspiracy Narratives in Roman History,* by Victoria Emma Pagán.

5. This phrase comes from Audre Lorde's essay "The Master's Tools Will Never Dismantle the Master's House" included in the 2020 collection *The Selected Works of Audre Lorde* edited by Roxane Gay.

6. For more information on how invasive species destabilize our human narratives about ecosystem health and resilience, read herbalist Timothy Lee Scott's book, *Invasive Plant Medicine: The Ecological Benefits and Healing Abilities of Invasives,* and Stephen Harrod Buhner's introduction to that book.

7. Toni Cade Bambara is quoted in adrienne maree brown's groundbreaking meditation on ecology and activism, *Emergent Strategy.*

14. REWILDING THE BELOVED: DIONYSUS OFFERS NEW MODES OF ROMANCE

1. This quotation is taken from the 2008 Ian Johnston translation of Euripides's play.

2. Scholar Elizabeth Wayland Barber charts the development of culture, storytelling, and women's social roles through the history of weaving in her 1996 book, *Women's Work: The First 20,000 Years: Women, Cloth, and Society in Early Times.*

3. The *Bibliotheca,* a first-century compendium of Greek myths, was originally thought to have been authored by Apollodorus. When that

authorship came into question, "Pseudo" was added to the attribution. The version quoted here is from Oxford World Classic's *The Library of Greek Mythology* translated by Robin Hard.

15. GROW BACK YOUR HORNS: THE DEVIL CARD IS DIONYSUS

1. Elaine Pagels is an authority on Gnosticism and early Christianity. Her 1979 book *The Gnostic Gospels* is generally accepted as the authoritative text on Gnostic Christianity and the Nag Hammadi scrolls. In *The Origin of Satan,* Pagels notes the evolution of the Hebrew term for "stumbling block" into the Koine Greek *skandalon,* meaning "snare" or "snag." Pagels shows that the word was used to describe early versions of devils. These "stumbling blocks" provided a course correction and kept someone from walking easily into sin. The original term holds no explicit moral baggage.

16. LET YOUR WINGS DRY: GIVING THE STAR CARD TO THE MASCULINE

1. Bonifacio Bembo was a fifteenth-century northern Italian artist commissioned by the Visconti-Sforza families to produce what is widely considered to be one of the first tarot decks. Not much is known about his background, but given the symbolic density of the illustrations, we can assume he had spiritual interests.
2. This poem is called "For the Interim Time" and is included in John O'Donohue's book of poems *To Bless the Space between Us.*
3. For a detailed photographic study of the dragonfly's transformation over its life cycle, visit the website of the British Dragonfly Society.

17. TRISTAN AND TRANSFORMATION: ESCAPING THE TRAUMA OF THE HERO'S JOURNEY

1. *Pharmakon* means simultaneously "medicine," "poison," and "drug." Philosophically, the term has been used to describe any object or idea whose dosage decides its classification.

2. German cleric Gottfried von Strassburg wrote his version of Tristan and Isolde at the beginning of the thirteenth century, basing it on the twelfth-century version by the poet known as Thomas of Britain. The work is unfinished, suggesting that von Strassburg died before its completion.

3. For a beginner's overview of somatics and how trauma registers in the body, read *The Body Keeps the Score,* by Bessel van der Kolk, and *Waking the Tiger,* by Peter Levine. For a peer-reviewed study on nervous system dysregulation and PTSD, consult the 2011 article "Post-Traumatic Stress Disorder: The Neurobiological Impact of Psychological Trauma," by J. E. Sherin and C. B. Nemeroff.

4. See, for example, *Staying with the Trouble: Making Kin in the Chthulucene* and other works by Donna Haraway.

18. BOY DAVID, WILD DAVID, KING DAVID: THE LAND-BASED ORIGIN OF BIBLICAL KINGSHIP

1. An expert on the Hebrew Bible, Graeme Auld notes in *Eerdmans Commentary on the Bible* that the offering of a silver-quarter shekel in Samuel 9 certainly fixes the composition of the text in the "Persian or Hellenistic Period because a quarter-shekel was known to exist in Hasmonean times." The rule of David is loosely dated to the tenth century BCE, far predating the creation of the Book of Samuel.

2. The Judaism of today bears little resemblance to the loosely assembled oral traditions of the warring tribes of early Israel. For an archaeological and historical perspective on the history of folkloric Judaism, see William G. Dever's 2005 book *Did God Have a Wife? Archaeology of Folk Religion in Ancient Israel.*

3. Robert Alter, a professor of comparative religion and Hebrew studies at the University of California, Berkeley, offers a nuanced and historically rich translation and interpretation of the David narrative in his 1999 book *The David Story.*

4. Lyres are among the world's oldest stringed instruments, with specimens

found in excavations in Ur (modern Iraq) dating back to 2500 BCE and the ancient Mesopotamian kingdom.

5. Campbell notes the iconographic similarities between David and Tristan in *Creative Mythology,* the final installment of his series, The Masks of God.

19. COPPICE THE HERO'S JOURNEY: CREATING NARRATIVE ECOSYSTEMS

1. Campbell popularized the monomythic concept of the hero's journey in his 1949 book *The Hero with a Thousand Faces.* While the narrative trope had already been investigated by anthropologist Edward Burnett Tylor and psychoanalyst Otto Rank, Campbell's formulation of seventeen stages of the monomyth quickly eclipsed earlier studies.

2. For an in-depth look at how egg choose sperm, see Carrie Arnold's 2017 article "Choosy Eggs May Pick Sperm for Their Genes, Defying Mendel's Law."

3. Neo-Darwinism is differentiated from Darwinism in that it expands and modifies Darwin's original theories, adding in gene theory and modern advances in biology.

4. American anthropologist Anna Lowenhaupt Tsing proposes "rubble ecologies" as a way of understanding complex, tangled systems of humans, animals, commerce, pollution, and violence in her 2015 book, *The Mushroom at the End of the World.*

5. Lynn Margulis edited *Symbiosis as a Source of Evolutionary Innovation* in 1991. An evolutionary biologist, she is famous for having theorized that symbiosis drives evolution. Her biggest contribution to modern biology is her discovery that our nucleic cells originate from the symbiogenetic fusion of separate organelles.

6. Anna Lowenhaupt Tsing's study of matsutake mushrooms in *The Mushroom at the End of the World* includes a textured analysis of Japan's satoyama forests.

20. MERLIN AND VORTIGERN:
MAGICAL BOYHOOD TOPPLES PATRIARCHY

1. Anne Baring and Jules Cashford offer a compelling argument for the conflation of snakes, monsters, and goddesses in their book *The Myth of the Goddess*.

2. Nikolai Tolstoy provides a rich interpretation of the history, texts, and locations associated with Merlin in his 1985 book *The Quest for Merlin*.

3. Known for his focus on landscape, travel, and language, in *Landmarks* Macfarlane salvages nature words that are currently falling out of use, meditating on how language brings us both closer to and farther away from our ecosystems.

21. PARZIFAL AND THE FISHER KING:
THE GRAIL OVERFLOWS WITH STORIES

1. German knight, musical composer, and poet Wolfram von Eschenbach based his romance on the earlier work of French poet Chrétien de Troyes. One of the first German versions of a Grail romance, *Parzifal* is one of the finest literary treatments of the Arthurian legends. Hundreds of years later, Richard Wagner would base his opera of the same title on von Eschenbach's work.

2. The passage can be read in full in Emma Jung and Marie-Louise von Franz's 1960 book *The Grail Legend*.

3. Poet Lyn Hejinian's meditation on closed and open texts can be found in her collection of essays *The Language of Inquiry*.

22. SLEEPING BEAUTY, SLEEPING WORLD:
THE PRINCE OFFERS THE MASCULINE
A NEW QUEST

1. Sola ratio is the Enlightenment understanding that it is by "reason alone" that we can make sense of reality. It represented the movement away from *sola scriptura*—using only scripture as guidance—into an increasingly secular view of science and nature.

2. The seventeenth-century French philosopher and scientist René Descartes is famous for the phrase "I think, therefore I am." He

influenced the recapitulation of the body/spirit dualism of Christianity into the mind/matter split of secular science. In Descartes' view, everything is a machine and the world is composed of automatons. Only human minds exist above and outside of this framework.

3. Charles Perrault was a seventeenth-century French author known for popularizing the modern conception of the fairy tale. He mined oral folklore and local stories to create his collection of tales, *Stories or Tales from Past Times, with Morals.*

24. RESURRECT THE BRIDEGROOM: THE SONG OF SONGS AND ECOLOGY AS COURTSHIP

1. The four canonical gospels that purport to tell the story of the life of Jesus were written many years and thousands of miles away from the historical reality of the man himself—and in the language of his executioners (Coptic Greek) no less. It is important to understand that the Gospels reflect the political and social agendas of Roman proto-Christians more than they do the perspective of an illiterate Galilean rabbi. This discrepancy is explored exhaustively in John Dominic Crossan's *The Historical Jesus: The Life of a Mediterranean Jewish Peasant,* Elaine Pagels's *The Gnostic Gospels,* and Karen Armstrong's *The Lost Art of Scripture.*

2. In *Animacies,* an interdisciplinary study drawing together sexuality, race, ecology, and matter, author Mel Y. Chen writes: "Animacy is shaped by what or who counts as human, and what or who does not."

3. To learn more about Margulis and her research, read her 1998 book, *Symbiotic Planet: A New Look at Evolution.*

4. Lichen has recently become a popular metaphor for nonnormative sexuality and partnerships. A wonderful treatment of the science and poetry of lichen is the 2015 paper, "Queer Theory for Lichen," by David Griffiths. For a better understanding of the origins of "lichenization," see the 2015 paper, "Lichenization: The Origins of a Fungal Life-Style," by David Hawksworth.

5. A detailed, historically accurate reimagining of the life of the Galilean

magician can be found in Bruce Chilton's 2000 book, *Rabbi Jesus: An Intimate Biography.*

25. OSIRIS:
THE ORIGINAL GREEN MAN

1. One of the best collections of Osiris imagery, legends, and historical analysis can be found in *Osiris: Egypt's Sunken Mysteries,* by Frank Goddio and David Fabre, created as a counterpart to the 2015 exhibit of the same name at the Arab World Institute in Paris, France.

2. This ancient fragment about "laughing" was included on page 74 in the chapter "Harvest and Homage" in the 2018 book, *Living with the Gods: On Beliefs and Peoples,* by British art historian and former museum director Neil MacGregor.

3. Overshadowed by her male peers Ezra Pound and T. S. Eliot, Hilda Doolittle, otherwise known as H.D., was one of the founders of the Imagist movement. Her work *Trilogy* is typically read as a civilian war poem, although its concerns are far ranging and deeply spiritual.

26. WHAT'S THE MATTER?:
A MYCELIAL INTERPRETATION OF THE
GOSPEL OF MARY MAGDALENE

1. The Gnostic Gospel of Mary is found in a fifth-century papyrus codex, written in Coptic, alongside other famous Gnostic tracts such as the Sophia of Jesus Christ and the Apocryphon of John. These texts can be found in *The Gnostic Bible,* edited by Willis Barnstone and Marvin Meyer.

2. The Gospel of Thomas is one of the oldest collections of the sayings of Jesus. A part of the 1945 Nag Hammadi discovery, the text is composed of riddles and sayings that, while similar to passages from the synoptic gospels, do not occur within a set narrative. Based on references to the gospel in letters, and a denunciation of it by Athanasius, bishop of Alexandria, scholars have postulated that the original could have been written as early as 60 CE.

3. For a complete collection of Gnostic texts paired with commentary, consult *The Gnostic Bible,* edited by Willis Barnstone and Marvin Meyer.

4. I am referring to the translation of the Gospel of Mary included in *The Gnostic Bible,* edited by Willis Barnstone and Marvin Meyer.

5. Canadian forest ecologist Suzanne Simard was one of the first scientists to show that mycorrhizal fungi transfer nutrients between plants. The story of her research is included in her 2021 memoir *Finding the Mother Tree.*

6. I am referring again to the translation of the Gospel of Mary included in *The Gnostic Bible,* edited by Willis Barnstone and Marvin Meyer.

27. KNOCK UPON YOURSELF: THE HIGH PRIESTESS WAKES UP THE MASCULINE

1. Rachel Pollack unpacks the symbolism of this word in her book *Seventy-Eight Degrees of Wisdom.*

2. This quotation can be found in the Gnostic Teachings of Silvanus, from the Nag Hammadi library. It has been dated to around 150 CE. The translation I am using comes from Elaine Pagels in her book *The Gnostic Gospels.*

28. THE KINGDOM OF ASTONISHMENT: GNOSTIC JESUS AND THE TRANSFORMATIVE POWER OF AWE

1. See, for example, *Ancient Christian Gospels: Their History and Development* and other works by Helmut Koester.

2. The Gospel of Thomas quotations in this chapter come from Willis Barnstone and Marvin Meyer's *The Gnostic Bible.*

3. For a more comprehensive explanation of how psychedelics work on the brain, see Michael Pollan's book *How to Change Your Mind* and the 2018 study, "Classic Hallucinogens and Mystical Experiences: Phenomenology and Neural Correlates," by Frederick S. Barrett and Roland R. Griffiths.

29. HEALING THE HEALER: DIONYSUS REWILDS JESUS

1. In 78 CE, almost contemporary with the life of Jesus, Pliny the Elder wrote of mustard greens in his *Natural History,* translated by John F. Healey: "It

grows entirely wild . . . when it has once been sown it is scarcely possible to get the place free of it, as the seed when it falls germinates at once."

2. In his 2016 book, *The Quest for Mary Magdalene,* Michael Haag assembles primary sources to paint a picture of Palestine in the Second Temple period. Much information about the climate and ecology of Judea and Galilee comes from Josephus, a Jewish historian and a contemporary of Jesus, who recorded detailed descriptions of vegetation and daily life.

3. In his 2020 book, *The Immortality Key,* Brian Muraresku argues that early Christianity was virtually identical to the cult of Dionysus, inheriting a fermented sacrament and the worship of a dying/resurrecting vegetal god.

30. MAKING AMENDS TO ATTIS AND ADONIS: NO GODS WERE KILLED IN THE MAKING OF THIS MYTH

1. This overlay is noted by historian William Anderson in his book *Green Man* and by Anne Baring and Jules Cashford in *The Myth of the Goddess*.

2. Joseph Campbell himself interprets dying and resurrecting gods as symbolic of seasonal, lunar, and astrological shifts; see his book *Occidental Mythology*.

3. The 2020 book, *Under a White Sky,* by environmental journalist Elizabeth Kolbert, investigates how man-made technological intervention creates cascading disasters, even as it attempts to fix ecological problems.

31. THE JOYFUL RESCUE: TOLKIEN'S EUCATASTROPHE AND THE ANTHROPOCENE

1. Author and scholar J. R. R. Tolkien first developed the idea of the eucatastrophe in his 1939 lecture "On Fairy-stories," which he delivered as an Andrew Lang Lecture at the University of St. Andrews in Scotland.

2. This quotation comes from Letter 89 in *The Letters of J. R. R. Tolkien,* edited by Humphrey Carpenter.

3. For a collection of feminist responses to the Anthropocene, read the 2017 book *Anthropocene Feminisms,* edited by Richard Grusin.

32. SHARING THE MEAL: TOM BOMBADIL OFFERS THE MASCULINE SAFE HAVEN

1. For the full passage, see Letter 89 in *The Letters of J. R. R. Tolkien.*
2. The French philosopher Gaston Bachelard is best known for his 1957 meditation on architecture and aesthetics, *The Poetics of Space.*

Bibliography

Abram, David. *Becoming Animal: An Earthly Cosmology.* New York: Random House, 2010.

Abram, David. *The Spell of the Sensuous.* New York: Random House, 1997.

Albrecht G., G. M. Sartore, L. Connor, et al. "Solastalgia: The Distress Caused by Environmental Change," *Australasian Psychiatry* 15, suppl. 1 (2007): S95–98.

Aliki. *A Weed Is a Flower: The Life of George Washington Carver.* New York: Aladdin, 1988.

Alter, Robert. *The David Story.* New York: W. W. Norton & Company, 1999.

Anderson, William. *Green Man: Archetypes of Our Oneness with the Earth.* London: HarperCollins, 1990.

Apollodorus. *The Library of Greek Mythology.* Translated by Robin Hard. Oxford: Oxford University Press, 2008.

Armstrong, Karen. *The Lost Art of Scripture: Rescuing the Ancient Texts.* New York: Alfred A. Knopf, 2019.

Arnold, Carrie. "Choosy Eggs May Pick Sperm for Their Genes, Defying Mendel's Law." *Quanta Magazine,* November 15, 2017.

Aslan, Reza. *Zealot: The Life and Times of Jesus of Nazareth.* New York: Random House, 2013.

Astour, Michael C. *Hellenosemitica: An Ethnic and Cultural Study of West Semitic Impact on Mycenaean Greece.* Leiden, Netherlands: E. J. Brill, 1965.

Auld, Graeme. "1 and 2 Samuel." In *Eerdmans Commentary on the Bible,* edited by James D. G. Dunn and John William Rogerson, 213–245. Grand Rapids, Mich.: Eerdmans, 2003.

Bachelard, Gaston. *The Poetics of Space.* Boston: Beacon Press, 1969.

Barber, Elizabeth Wayland. *Women's Work: The First 20,000 Years.* New York: W. W. Norton, 1996.

Baring, Anne, and Jules Cashford. *The Myth of the Goddess: Evolution of an Image.* London: Penguin Books, 1991.

Barnstone, Willis, and Marvin Meyer. *The Gnostic Bible: Gnostic Texts of Mystical Wisdom from the Ancient and Medieval Worlds.* Boston: Shambhala, 2009.

Barrett, Frederick S., and Roland R. Griffiths. "Classic Hallucinogens and Mystical Experiences: Phenomenology and Neural Correlates." *Current Topics in Behavioral Neurosciences* 36 (2018): 393–430.

Bedier, Jospeh. *The Romance of Tristan and Iseut.* Translated by Edward J. Gallagher. Indianapolis: Hackett Publishing Company, 2013.

Bierend, Doug. *In Search of Mycotopia: Citizen Science, Fungi, Fanatics, and the Untapped Potential of Mushrooms.* White River Junction, Vt.: Chelsea Green Publishing, 2021.

Bone, Eugenia. *Mycophilia: Revelations from the Weird World of Mushrooms.* New York: Rodale, 2011.

Borg, Marcus. *The Lost Gospel Q: The Original Sayings of Jesus.* Berkeley: Ulysses Press, 1999.

Borissoff, Constaine L. "Non-Iranian Origin of the Eastern-Slavonic God Xursu/Xors." *Studia Mythologica Slavica* 17 (2014): 9–36.

Bringhurst, Robert. *Everywhere Being Is Dancing: Twenty Pieces of Thinking.* Berkeley: Counterpoint, 2008.

———. *The Tree of Meaning: Language, Mind, and Ecology.* Berkeley: Counterpoint, 2008.

brown, adrienne maree. *Emergent Strategy: Shaping Change, Changing Worlds.* Chico, Calif.: Akashic Press, 2017.

Brundrett, Mark C. "Coevolution of Roots and Mycorrhizas of Land Plants." *New Phytologist* 154, no. 2 (2002): 275–304.

Buhner, Stephen Harrod: *Plant Intelligence and the Imaginal Realm: Into the Dreaming of Earth.* Rochester, Vt.: Bear & Company, 2014.

Campbell, Joseph. *Creative Mythology.* The Masks of God, vol. 4. New York: Penguin Books, 1968.

———. *The Hero with a Thousand Faces.* New York: Princeton University Press, 1973.

———. *Occidental Mythology.* The Masks of God, vol. 3. New York: Penguin Books, 1964.

Candeias, Matt. *In Defense of Plants: An Exploration into the Wonder of Plants.* Coral Gables, Fl.: Mango Publishing Group, 2021.

Chen, Mel Y. *Animacies: Biopolitics, Racial Mattering, and Queer Affect.* Durham, N. C. and London: Duke University Press, 2012.

Chilton, Bruce. *Rabbi Jesus: An Intimate Biography.* New York: Doubleday Broadway Publishing, 2000.

Crossan, John Dominic. *The Historical Jesus: The Life of a Mediterranean Jewish Peasant.* San Francisco: HarperOne, 1993.

Darwin, Charles, and Francis Darwin. *The Power of Movement in Plants.* New York: Cosimo Classics, 1880.

Davies, Sioned, trans. *The Mabinogion.* Oxford: Oxford University Press, 2008.

Dever, William G. *Did God Have a Wife? Archaeology and Folk Religion in Ancient Israel.* Grand Rapids, Mich.: William B. Erdman's Publishing Company, 2005.

Doolittle, Hilda [H.D.]. *Trilogy.* New York: New Directions Books, 1998.

Ehrenreich, Barbara. "'Humans Were Not Centre Stage': How Ancient Cave Art Puts Us in Our Place." *The Guardian,* December 12, 2019.

Eisler, Riane. *The Chalice and the Blade: Our History, Our Future.* San Francisco: HarperOne, 1988.

Euripides. *Bacchae.* Translated by Ian Johnston. Arlington, Va.: Richer Resources Publication, 2008.

———. *The Bacchae.* Translated by Gilbert Murray. Overland Park, Kans.: Digireads.com Publishing, 2019.

———. *Bakkhai.* Translated by Anne Carson. New York: New Directions, 2015.

Eschenbach, Wolfram von. *Parzifal.* Translated by A. T. Hatto. New York: Penguin, 1980.

Geoffrey of Monmouth. *The History of the Kings of Britain.* Translated by Lewis Thorpe. London: Penguin Classics, 1977.

———. *Vita Merlini.* Translated by John Jay Perry. [orig. pub. ca. 1150].

Ghosh, Amitav. *The Great Derangement: Climate Change and the Unthinkable.* Chicago: University of Chicago Press, 2016.

Gilbert, K. J., L. S. Bittleston, W. Tong, et al. "Tropical Pitcher Plants *(Nepenthes)* Act as Ecological Filters by Altering Properties of Their Fluid Microenvironments." *Scientific Reports* 10, no. 4431 (2020).

Gillette, Douglas, and Robert Moore. *King, Warrior, Magician, Lover: Rediscovering the Archetypes of the Mature Masculine.* New York: HarperCollins, 1990.

Gimbutas, Marija. *The Living Goddesses.* Berkeley: University of California Press, 2001.

Goddio, Frank, and David Fabre. *Osiris: Egypt's Sunken Mysteries.* Paris: Flammarion, 2018.

Goodrich, Norma Lorre. *Merlin.* New York: Harper & Rowe Publishers, 1988.

Griffiths, David. "Queer Theory for Lichens." *UnderCurrents: Journal of Critical Environmental Studies* 19 (2015): 36–45.

Grusin, Richard, ed. *Anthropocene Feminisms.* Minneapolis: University of Minnesota, 2017.

Guggenheim, Alena G., Kirsten M. Wright, and Heather L. Zwickey. "Immune Modulation from Five Major Mushrooms: Application to Integrative Oncology" *Integrative Medicine* 13 (2014): 32–44.

Haag, Michael. *The Quest for Mary Magdalene.* New York: Harper Paperbacks, 2016.

Haraway, Donna J. *Staying with the Trouble: Making Kin in the Chthulucene.* Durham, N. C. and London: Duke University Press, 2016.

Hassett, Maribeth O., Mark W. F. Fischer, and Nicholas P. Money. "Mushrooms as Rainmakers: How Spores Act as Nuclei for Raindrops." *PLoS ONE* 10, no. 10 (2015): e0140407.

Hawksworth, David. "Lichenization: The Origins of a Fungal Life-Style." *Recent Advances in Lichenology: Modern Methods and Approaches in Lichen Systematics and Culture Techniques* 2 (February 2015): 1–10.

Hejinian, Lyn. *The Language of Inquiry*. Berkeley: University of California Press, 2000.

Judson A. P. "The Mystery of the Mycenaean 'Labyrinth': The Value of Linear B *Pu₂* and Related Signs." *SMEA NS* 3 (2017): 53–72.

Jung, Emma, and Marie-Louise von Franz. *The Grail Legend*. Princeton: Princeton University Press, 1998 [orig. pub. 1960].

Kenrick, Paul, and Christine Strullu-Derrien. "The Origin and Early Evolution of Roots." *Plant Physiology* 166, no. 2 (2014): 570–80.

Kerényi, Carl. *Dionysos: Archetypal Image of Indestructible Life*. Translated by Ralph Menheim. Princeton: Princeton University Press, 1976.

Kern, Otto. *Orphicorum Fragmenta, collegit*. Berlin: Apud Weidmannos, 1922.

Kimmerer, Robin Wall. *Braiding Sweetgrass: Indigenous Wisdom, Scientific Knowledge, and the Teachings of Plants*. Minneapolis: Milkweed Editions, 2013.

Knohl, Israel. "Joseph and the Famine: The Story's Origins in Egyptian History." TheTorah.com, December 26, 2019.

Koester, Helmut. *Ancient Christian Gospels: Their History and Development*. Harrisburg, Pa.: Trinity Press International, 1992.

Kolbert, Elizabeth. *Under a White Sky: The Nature of the Future*. New York: Penguin Random House, 2021.

Kolk, Bessel van der. *The Body Keeps the Score: Brain, Mind, and Body in the Healing of Trauma*. New York: Viking, 2014.

Leeman, Diane. "Apotropaic Wands of the Middle Kingdom." Academia.edu, 2019.

Leuchter, Mark. "Genesis 38 in Social and Historical Perspective." *Journal of Biblical Literature* 132, no. 2 (2013): 209–27.

Levine, Peter A. with Anna Frederick. *Waking the Tiger: Healing Trauma*. Berkeley: North Atlantic Books, 1997.

Lewis, C. S. *On Stories and Other Essays on Literature*. New York: Harcourt Brace Jovanavich, 1982.

Lorde, Audre. *The Selected Works of Audre Lorde*. Edited by Roxane Gay. London: W. W. Norton & Company, 2020.

Lovelock, James. *The Revenge of Gaia*. London: Penguin Books, 2007.

Macfarlane, Robert. *Landmarks*. London: Penguin Books, 2016.

———. *Underland: A Deep Time Journey*. New York: W. W. Norton & Company, 2019.

MacGregor, Neil. *Living with the Gods: On Beliefs and Peoples*. New York: Alfred A. Knopf, 2018.

Magan, Manchán. *Thirty-Two Words for Field: Lost Words of the Irish Landscape*. Dublin: Gill Books, 2020.

Malhotra, Rajiv. *Indra's Net: Defending Hinduism's Philosophical Unity*. New York: HarperCollins, 2016.

Margulis, Lynn. *Symbiotic Planet: A New Look at Evolution*. New York: Basic Books, 1998.

Margulis, Lynn and René Fester, eds. *Symbiosis as a Source of Evolutionary Innovation: Speciation and Morphogenesis*. Cambridge: MIT Press, 1991.

Meyer, Marvin. *The Gospel of Thomas: The Hidden Sayings of Jesus*. New York: HarperSanFrancisco, 1992.

Morton, Timothy. *Dark Ecology: For a Logic of Future Coexistence*. New York: Columbia University Press, 2016.

Muraresku, Brian. *The Immortality Key: The Secret History of the Religion with No Name*. New York: St. Martin's Press, 2020.

Nock, A. D. "Notes on Ruler-Cult, I–IV." *The Journal of Hellenic Studies* 48, no. 1 (1928): 21–43.

O'Donohue, John. *To Bless the Space between Us: A Book of Blessings*. New York: Doubleday Broadway Publishing, 2008.

Ovid. *Metamorphoses*. Translated by David Raeburn. London: Penguin Classics, 2004.

Pagels, Elaine. *Adam, Eve, and the Serpent*. New York: Random House, 1988.

———. *The Gnostic Gospels*. New York: Random House, 1979.

———. *The Origin of Satan*. New York: Random House, 1995.

Pendell, Dale. *Pharmako/Poeia: Plant Powers, Poisons & Herbcraft*. Berkeley: North Atlantic Books, 1995.

Perrault, Charles. *The Complete Fairy Tales*. Translated by Christopher Betts. Oxford: Oxford University Press, 2010.

Platon, Nikolaos. *Guide to the Archaeological Museum of Heraclion*. Heraklion, Crete: 1955.

Pliny the Elder. *Natural History: A Selection.* Translated by John F. Healey. New York: Penguin Random House, 1991.

Plutarch. *Lives, Vol. III, Pericles and Fabius Maximus. Nicias and Crassus.* Translated by Bernadotte Perrin. Cambridge: Harvard University Press, 1916.

Pollack, Rachel. *Seventy-Eight Degrees of Wisdom: A Tarot Journey to Self-Awareness.* Newburyport, Mass.: Weiser Books, 2019.

Pollan, Michael. *How to Change Your Mind: What the New Science of Psychedelics Teaches Us about Consciousness, Dying, Addiction, Depression, and Transcendence.* New York: Penguin Press, 2018.

Rilke, Rainer Maria. *Ahead of All Parting: The Selected Poetry and Prose of Rainer Maria Rilke.* Translated by Stephen Mitchell. New York: Modern Library, 1995.

Salmón, Enrique. "Kincentric Ecology: Indigenous Perceptions of the Human Nature." *Ecological Applications* 10, no. 5 (2000): 1327–32.

———. *Iwigara: The Kinship of Plants and People.* Portland, Ore.: Timber Press, 2020.

Schama, Simon. *The Story of the Jews: Finding the Words.* New York: HarperCollins, 2013.

Schmitt, Craig L., and Michael L. Tatum. *The Malheur National Forest: Location of the World's Largest Living Organism [The Humongous Fungus].* United States Department of Agriculture, Forest Service, Pacific Northwest Region, 2008.

Scott, Timothy Lee. *Invasive Plant Medicine: The Ecological Benefits and Healing Abilities of Invasives.* Rochester, Vt.: Healing Arts Press, 2010.

Sheldrake, Merlin. *Entangled Life: How Fungi Make Our Worlds, Change Our Minds & Shape Our Futures.* New York: Random House, 2020.

Sheldrake, Rupert. *Science Set Free: 10 Paths to New Discovery.* New York: Deepak Chopra Books, 2012.

Sherin, J. E., and C. B. Nemeroff. "Post-Traumatic Stress Disorder: The Neurobiological Impact of Psychological Trauma." *Dialogues in Clinical Neuroscience* 13, no. 3 (2011): 263–78.

Shlain, Leonard. *The Alphabet versus the Goddess: The Conflict between Word and Image.* New York: Viking Arkana, 1998.

Simard, Suzanne. *Finding the Mother Tree: Discovering the Wisdom of the Forest.* New York: Alfred A. Knopf, 2021.

Sjöö, Monica, and Barbara Mor. *The Great Cosmic Mother: Rediscovering the Religion of the Earth.* San Francisco: HarperOne, 1987.

Stamets, Paul. *Mycelium Running: How Mushrooms Can Help Save the World.* New York: Penguin Random House, 2005.

Stengers, Isabelle. *Cosmopolitics I.* Translated by Robert Bononno. Minneapolis: University of Minnesota Press, 2010.

Strassburg, Gottfried von. *Tristan: With Surviving Fragments of the "Tristan of Thomas."* Translated by A. T. Hatto. London: Penguin Classics, 1960.

Taylor, Thomas, trans. *The Orphic Hymns.* [orig. pub. 1824 as *The Mystical Hymns of Orpheus.*]

Telushkin, Rabbi Joseph. *Biblical Literacy.* New York: William Morrow and Company, 1997.

Tolkien, J. R. R. *The Letters of J. R. R. Tolkien.* Edited by Humphrey Carpenter. New York: William Morrow, 2000.

———. *The Lord of the Rings: One Volume Edition.* London: HarperCollins, 1994.

———. *Tolkien On Fairy-stories.* Edited by Verlyn Flieger and Douglas A. Anderson. New York: HarperCollins, 2014.

Tolstoy, Nikolai. *The Quest for Merlin.* London: Little, Brown and Company, 1985.

Trzaskoma, Stephen M., R. Scott Smith, and Stephen Brunet. *Anthology of Classical Myth: Primary Sources in Translation.* Indianapolis: Hackett Publishing Company, 2004.

Tsing, Anna Lowenhaupt. *The Mushroom at the End of the World: On the Possibility of Life in Capitalist Ruins.* Princeton: Princeton University Press, 2015.

Tsing, Anna, Heather Swanson, Elaine Gan, and Nils Bubandt, eds. *Arts of Living on a Damaged Planet.* Minneapolis: University of Minnesota Press, 2017.

Whatham, A. E. "The Yahweh-Tehom Myth." *The Biblical World* 36, no. 5 (1910): 329–333.

Whyte, David. *Consolations: The Solace, Nourishment and Underlying Meaning of Everyday Words*. Edinburgh: Canongate Press, 2019.

Yong, Ed. *I Contain Multitudes: The Microbes within Us and a Grander View of Life*. New York: HarperCollins, 2016.

Yunkaporta, Tyson. *Sand Talk: How Indigenous Thinking Can Save the World*. Melbourne, Australia: Text Publishing, 2019.

Zwicky, Jan, and Robert Bringhurst. *Learning to Die: Wisdom in the Age of Climate Crisis*. Saskatchewan, Canada: University of Regina Press, 2018.

Index